Men Still in Exile

Edited by Michele Dishong McCormack

Men Still in Exile
ISBN: 978-1-943536-40-5

Chemeketa Press

Chemeketa Press is a nonprofit publishing endeavor at Chemeketa Community College that works with faculty, staff, and students to create affordable and effective alternatives to commercial textbooks. All proceeds from the sales of this book go toward the development of new books. To learn more, visit www.chemeketapress.org.

Publisher: Tim Rogers
Managing Editor: Steve Richardson
Production Editor: Brian Mosher
Instructional Editor: Stephanie Lenox
Design Editor: Ronald Cox IV

Cover Art: Tanager, by Francisco Hernandez

Printed in the United States of America.

This book is dedicated to Nancy Green.

"For I was hungry and you gave me something to eat, I was thirsty and you gave me something to drink, I was a stranger and you invited me in, I needed clothing and you clothed me, I was sick and you looked after me, I was in prison and you looked after me." — Jesus of Nazareth

Your treasure can never be taken. Thank you for everything.

Contents

Editor's Note xiii

Introduction 1

Gratitude and Faith

Distorted Innocence — Charles C. Hammond II 5

A Life Awash in Birds — Michele Dishong McCormack 7

Great Blue — Francisco Hernandez 9

Commencement Speech — Phillip 10

Depression — HJ Walker 12

Grateful and Blessed — Brandon Davila 14

Gratitude — Francisco Hernandez 16

Tanager — Francisco Hernandez 17

Over the Years — Phillip 18

Thankful — Nestor Diaz-Miller 19

Through the Bars — Francisco Hernandez 21

Cardinal at Rest — Francisco Hernandez 22

We Don't Believe in That — SP 23

Who Am I — Benjamin James Hall 27

Hopes and Dreams

Future Encounter — Charles C. Hammond II 31

The Doorway to Nowhere — Charles C. Hammond II 32

Criminals and Teddy Bears — HJ Walker 34

Discovery of Self — HJ Walker 36

Dream — Brandon Davila 39

Dream Big!!! — Brandon Davila 41

Emotional Garbage — SP.. 42

Hope's Highway — Benjamin James Hall.................................. 44

Mercy — Francisco Hernandez 46

My Window — Francisco Hernandez 51

Winter Swan — Francisco Hernandez 52

Patience — Phillip 53

Exit Interview — Phillip.. 54

The Moon Through the Bars — Benjamin James Hall................ 58

The New Unwanted — Francisco Hernandez 60

Today — Brandon Davila 63

Inside

Fear, Chains, and Ankle Irons — James M. Anderson 67

Full Moon — HJ Walker 75

Human — Francisco Hernandez................................. 80

Life — Phillip 81

Lockdown — Benjamin James Hall 82

National Anthems — Michele Dishong McCormack 84

9/11/2011 — Benjamin James Hall............................. 88

Rehabilitation — HJ Walker 91

Silent Cries — Benjamin James Hall............................ 92

The Conclusion — SP 95

Beyond the Wall — Francisco Hernandez....................... 96

The Creature — Nestor Diaz-Miller 97

The Phone Rings — Benjamin James Hall.................... 99

Wasteland — Benjamin James Hall............................ 101

Love

#19 — Brandon Davila 105

Brick by Brick — Nestor Diaz-Miller 107

Fusion — Francisco Hernandez 109

I Want — Brandon Davila 110

meditate — kosal so 111

My Wine — Nestor Diaz-Miller 113

Unconventional Fairy Tale — Nestor Diaz-Miller 114

The Room — Nestor Diaz-Miller 116

the war of beauty — kosal so 118

This Sky of Ours — Nestor Diaz-Miller 119

Mom and Family

Chimes in the Wind — Charles C. Hammond II 123

A Mother's Love — Charles C. Hammond II 125

The Answer on the Other End of the Phone —
Charles C. Hammond II 126

Better — Charles C. Hammond II 128

My Most Cherished Moment Is… —
Charles C. Hammond II 129

A Father's Love — HJ Walker 132

A Mother's Heart — Benjamin James Hall 135

Best Friend — Nestor Diaz-Miller 137

A Letter to Mom — HJ Walker 139

Hero — HJ Walker 140

homage to her feet — kosal so 142

Knock on Heaven's Door — HJ Walker 144

Letters — Francisco Hernandez 145

Looking Over the Wall — Francisco Hernandez 147

Meeting Jackie — Benjamin James Hall 149

Momma Knows Best — Brandon Davila 151

My Forgotten Aunt — SP 152

Other Mothers' Sons — Michele Dishong McCormack 155

The Gift of Discovery — James M. Anderson 156

Time Bomb — Brandon Davila 164

Other Thoughts

Blah Blah's — Charles C. Hammond II 169

Under the Surface — Charles C. Hammond II 170

A World I Call My Own — SP 171

Alone — Jon Killoran 174

An Induced Mind — SP 176

Earthquake Drills — Jon Killoran 181

Existentialism — Jon Killoran 183

Ink is Thicker... — Brandon Davila 184

Light — Francisco Hernandez 186

lightness of being — kosal so 187

Lock Them Up and Throw Away the Keys — HJ Walker 188

More at 11 — Jon Killoran 190

My Noninvasive Procedure — SP 192

playing god — kosal so 194

rimes of salt — kosal so 196

running water — kosal so 197

Say What? — Jon Killoran 199

Sayings That Shouldn't Make Sense — Jon Killoran 201

Staring is Always Creepy — Jon Killoran 203

The Battle — SP 204

The Big Book of Cynical Philosophy — Jon Killoran 205

which god? — kosal so 208

Regrets

Home Town — Charles C. Hammond II 211

10 p.m. Endless Climb — Benjamin James Hall 213

California Son — Phillip 215

Fertility — James M. Anderson 216

From the Start — James M. Anderson 218

Listen! — Benjamin James Hall 221

sandcastles — kosal so 223

held reservoir — kosal so 225

Thunder and Rain — James M. Anderson 226

Time — James M. Anderson 228

Where Were You Last Night? — Nestor Diaz-Miller 230

Whisper to a Roar — Nestor Diaz-Miller 233

Who Would Have Known? — James M. Anderson 235

Acknowledgments 237

Author Biographies 239

Editor's Note

"Poets and writers have been civilizing the inhabitants of the planet Earth for centuries. Some voices have been heard and neglected. To the extent that we delay hearing the voices from prison, to precisely that extent do we delay civilization." — Justice Bruce McM. Wright

Through the Chapel Library's tall, drafty wall of windows, I look out over Mill Creek and a nondescript industrial slice of Salem, Oregon. Behind me, shelves of books and nature murals on three walls provide respite inside a 167-year-old fortress. Here I set up my weekly creative writing class. The writers arrive with their yellow authorization slips, and the door is closed. We are now in a cocoon of sorts, an offbeat refuge adorned with books, art, random bits of electronics, misshapen meditation cushions, and thick, dark blankets perched on top of sturdy locked cabinets. Beyond all this stretches the beige-drab, 30-foot wall of the Oregon State Penitentiary.

Above my students' heads, stenciled bright red and black letters on white ceiling pipes warn "not to make dust" because of asbestos. We would rather write than make dust in this space, prime real estate that we are blessed to have, thanks to the chaplains and other supporters over the years. There is a softness here, which contrasts with the clanging gates of metal, acres of echoing concrete, swaths of linoleum, and squawk of loudspeakers on the other side. The context shifts here, cushioned by a feeling of peace, custom window coverings, and blue starburst carpet.

This sacred space provides sanctuary for the essays, poems, and artwork in this book, from voices that aren't widely heard but sometimes emerge from this cocoon. As one of the writers puts it: "We want the world to know that there is a community of men inside these walls who are more than just prisoners."

The Penned Thoughts writers group formed in November 2008, shortly after I met two men, James and Josh, during my first-ever prison visit. I was there with other donors for a ceremony celebrating the accomplishments of incarcerated Chemeketa Community College students. James shocked me that day when he said he'd lived at the penitentiary for ten years (since he was seventeen) with no hope, other than regular visits with his mom and other loved ones, until he began to take college classes. Josh, who coined our Penned Thoughts group name, just earned his bachelor's degree, a dream he told me about early on. At that time, I didn't think that earning a bachelor's degree inside prison could happen.

I felt the men's urgency to write that first day with the arrival of Josh, James, and seventeen other men. The group's membership has changed over time due to work schedules, prison transfers, release dates, and other factors, but the sense of community remains. Writers use words like "magical sanctuary" and "safe place" to describe our group, which meets for two hours nearly every Wednesday morning and for sometimes longer sessions to host guest writers who are always surprised by how engaged and talented the writers are.

The men's work has been shared on national websites and at literary readings. A spring 2013 event involved my reading some of the men's writing during a conference sponsored by the United Nations. Some of the work has also been shared at annual readings for the writers' friends and families. The writers have attended workshops with prison activist Sister Helen Prejean and other regionally and nationally known authors, such as Craig Lancaster, Naseem Rakha, Lauren Kessler, Matt Love, and Maggie Powers. The men's work gained international exposure after a spring 2017 reading and workshop with Stacey Astill, who was the Isle of Man's National Bard that year

The book now in your hands joins *Ebb & Flow: Writings from Penned Thoughts*, a previously released collection of essays, poems, and artwork. Men currently housed in four prisons and two who have been released have joined forces on *Men Still in Exile*, the publication of which coincides with the group's tenth anniversary. I hope that each reader will find something to resonate with him or her, and in reading this collection will realize that the artists and writers featured are someone's father, son, uncle, husband, neighbor. They are athletes and rappers, painters and carvers, hospice volunteers and musicians.

I've also had a wide variety of jobs, which include waitress, ranch cook, congressional speechwriter, radio reporter, marketing director, and teacher, but the most rewarding work I've ever undertaken is inside prison walls. The writers' group led me to teach for Chemeketa Community College's College Inside program, advocate and testify at the legislature for prison education, serve as a facilitator for the Alternatives to Violence Project, deliver classes in the internationally recognized Inside-Out model, and teach and work with a University of Oregon team of students, alumni, and professors. These endeavors fall in line with theologian Frederick Buechner's idea that one's calling comes from the place "where your deep gladness and the world's deep hunger meet." This certainly feels like a calling to me and one I would've never predicted. I will always be in debt to Nancy Green, my mentor, colleague, and dear friend, for leading me to this place.

I also hope that the writers featured in this book and the other men I've met at five Oregon prisons deeply know that working, learning, volunteering, serving, and teaching alongside them has been one of the most significant privileges of my life. These men will always have a place in my heart, mind, writing, and activism. I hope readers will see at least some of what I see: people who are compassionate, kind, and caring; people who have made mistakes and have overcome challenges; people who love their families and who desire opportunities for change; people whose stories of love, loss, hope, and regret offer a meaningful glimpse inside our common struggle.

— Michele Dishong McCormack

Introduction

In prison, specific dates and times are often hazy. Months and years are coalesced between a life marked by seasons or events.

Penned Thoughts writing group was formed in 2008 after a kind-hearted speech teacher visited a place many never imagine themselves going: the penitentiary. Most of us spend our days dreaming of breaking out of this context in which we reside, but this speech teacher and writer from Nebraska figured a way to break in and is now a part of this shared context with us.

Penned Thoughts is so much more than a writing group; it is a sacred place full of authenticity, creativity, and shared life that is carried far outside these prison walls. In the winter of 2011 we produced our first anthology *Ebb & Flow: Writings from Penned Thoughts*.

One of the events jumbled between now and then was the discovery of a book titled *Men in Exile*. Now out of print, this book was published in 1973 and its authors were men incarcerated in the Oregon State Penitentiary, where we currently reside. The book is full of stories and poetry; rich poetry permeated the book by an author known as Smokey, and a story, among others, of a monk from Mt. Angel who went outside the simplicity of his lifelong vow to visit a prisoner. We talked about how much the dynamics of prison had changed since then with mass incarceration, mental health issues, and gangs.

Through much discussion, the idea to write an unofficial sequel to this book is now coming to fruition. In the following pages are our words, stories, and poems filled with hopes, sorrows, laughter, and a context which touches the universal and the eternal: our humanity.

We are Men Still in Exile, but our hearts are not restrained, nor are they barren of that deep imaginative aptitude of the soul where ideas abide, which all human beings possess.

— Benjamin James Hall

Gratitude and Faith

Charles C. Hammond II

Distorted Innocence

I awoke in a cold sweat, barely aware of where I was or why I couldn't shake the images that seared me to the core. It was a dream like no other that I experienced, and one that I will never forget for the rest of my days.

It began like many others before it, but I soon learned that any such similarities ended there. I found myself walking down a side street of a nameless city. Unsure of my direction, I felt compelled to walk the line in the center of the street. It was just after daybreak. Both sides of the street were busy with the morning commute to and from each appointed destiny. My eyes were fixed upon the road ahead that stretched deep into the heart of the city, unfazed by the movement on either side of me as I continued forward without a pre-determined destination.

Ahead in the distance, a small boy riding his bright red tricycle weaved his way in and out between those passing by, ringing his shiny new bell that rested atop the tasseled handlebars announcing his presence. My attention now fully rested upon this bold young boy headed my way and I noticed that he was the only image. With every stroke of his pedals, the beat of my heart raced in anticipation of what I was about to see. After what felt like an eternity in slow motion, he came to a stop directly across from where I stood.

Unhindered by the blur of those passing by, he turned his gaze towards me as if to look down into my soul. Unable to look away or to even move, I took in every detail searching for what he may have held for me. Immediately, I was drawn to his eyes, but instead of the radiance of a child's innocence I saw the brick wall behind him through where his eyes should have been. With a slight hesitation, he turned back towards his destination, off again as if nothing was amiss. Unsure of what I had just witnessed, I looked back for one last look; what I saw changed me forever. From head to toe he looked like an empty shell, charred and spent with no substance, not unlike the view that you would see as you looked to the backside of a mask: carved out and featureless. Then those going about their business in oblivion come into focus to show their own state.

They were all the same, smoldering from the inside out permeating the air with the stench of sulfur, walking numbly seeking to fill the insatiable void that they fed daily, finding nothing that could possibly make them whole. Their eyes burned out and empty, one after another seeing nothing but an illusion of life spent in an endless search of what they do not know, just that they are compelled to seek.

All at once things began to become clear, the state of those in search of what was once placed deep within all man at the beginning of creation has manifested itself to reveal the true nature of the lost in need of what only God can replenish, a charred remnant of a once cherished life. It has been said that many are called, but few have been chosen, so choose well, lest you become as those whose eyes are seared black as night, walking numbly and unaware.

Michele Dishong McCormack

A Life Awash in Birds

*For all of the writers, past and present, in the Penned Thoughts writers'
group at the Oregon State Penitentiary*

A congregation of egrets,
looking down from a lopsided fir,
ushered me from Coos Bay
toward a new-old life,
white-hot fissures of failure
already forming.

A flock of pigeons
strung like faded, fat clothespins
on telephone wire
welcomed me:
1950s cottage
with its large yard, crazy plantings,
and drug house down the street.

A charm of finches
chirped outside as the baby
cried, ate, sang, crawled.
He's upright now, in second grade:
my son, one of two vital passions.
A murder of crows
keeping careful watch

over my other passion
notes my progress into
the yellow-drab,
concertina-festooned warehouse.

Here I stand, on a perch of sorts,
with my Penned Thoughts,
tending to a calling
ushered forth from:

A congregation of egrets,
A flock of pigeons,
A charm of finches,
A murder of crows, and

A prison chapel cage of jailbirds
flying toward freedom
through the quills of their pens.

Francisco Hernandez

Great Blue

Phillip

Commencement Speech

Hello my name is Phil; I have a few, heartfelt words I would like to say:

My friends and family are exceptionally proud of my accomplishments; inmates from other prisons that I've known over the years have written to me and said that they are proud of me as well. The single, burning thought that I need to say is, "Thank you!"

It has taken years of dedication to accomplish this, not just on my part, but on the part of many other people behind the scenes that are truly responsible for me standing before you. They also have selflessly dedicated years of helping and guiding me to this point in my life.

You have all heard the phrase "it takes a village to raise a child"? That is a catchy phrase, and until recently that's all it was to me, a catchy phrase. However, as of late, that simple phrase has taken on meaning in my life. I now have a personal understanding as to the simple truth of that phrase.

I attended Los Angeles County Unified School District growing up. There were gang fights, shootings, and stabbings; sometimes that was before lunch. I had numerous teachers say to me, "If you don't want to show up for class you don't have to. I'll check you off and you won't fail." And, true to their word, I passed the classes. However, I did fail because they failed me! What that entire environment prepared me for was a life of recklessness and prison.

Despite my murky background, here I am in prison, standing before you as a Chemeketa Community College Graduate. I did not get here on my own. It was definitely not an easy undertaking for me. It took numerous dedicated teachers coming into a prison to teach me. These selfless teachers gave me more than I've ever received in my life.

Their dedication, understanding, patience, and motivation kept me on a dedicated path to this very point. What can you say to the courage of these people that do this?

Thank You seems so inadequate. Yet, that is all I have, the most sincere, heartfelt Thank You that I can recall ever saying.

You teachers gave me my life. It also took many students to help tutor me.

This says a lot for the character building that the Chemeketa staff instills to the teachers and students; they are dedicated to our success.

This is the village. Teachers, fellow inmates, all coming together to guide, assist, and push me and many others down this path of growth and accomplishment.

As I've sat through graduations and been proud of those who have graduated before me, I am now proud to be before those who will graduate after me, knowing that they too will be where I am this day.

This program is preparing me to become a productive member of society upon my release.

I owe this once-in-a-lifetime opportunity to the Anonymous Donor and Nancy Green. Without your dedication and generosity, this would not have been possible.

For what you have done for me, I feel a responsibility to not let you down.

You have selflessly given me the keys to my own life. Thank You so much; I'm proud to be part of this village. And what's more, I'm grateful that you are part of this village.

HJ Walker

Depression

My horizon darkens with the blackest of clouds. My body melts in fatigue at the thought of the storm coming. Always frozen in fear with no place to hide from what is coming.

Depression is like the wind, coming and going at its own pleasure. Like a wreck on a four-lane highway. I can be just cruising along, perhaps humming a favorite song, when in an instant my world is turned upside down. The red in my rosy day is now blood spilled on the hot black top. Broken glass and twisted shards of angry metal. My favorite song now just screams of sirens.

I am weary from the fight, having to box in the air at an opponent I can't see. An imbalance of chemical reactions, that collides on the highway on my mind. With each bout I swear to train better for the next round, but no defense has yet been able to stop the onslaught. Round after round depression penetrates with knockout blows.

Every waking moment is spent catering to its desires to wreak havoc. Prison feeds it with the energy of darkness and despair. All around are lives of mental illnesses, each foraging upon violence. Everyday is a tangle of personalities. Loved ones and friends affected through visits, letters and phone calls by the chaos.

Diets, exercise programs, prayer groups and meditation sessions. I just want to scream, tear up my Bible, crawl in my bunk and withdraw from the world. Wrestling with thoughts of unworthiness is a chess game of mental exhaustion. I beg for sleep only to find more of this day-time nightmare. One, two, three days, surely an end must be in sight.

What are my alternatives? Drugs are always the promised cure; however I waver in indecision, should I make an appointment with the Mental Health Department? I fear complicating my life with further insanities. I've seen the effects on others who have chosen that pathway. Inmates in the psych unit that have lost touch with reality due to drug complications. Souls that are on permanent vacation, but who never left the farm.

I am quite aware of my sometime multiple personalities. Unsure at times what roller coaster ride you will get, but no matter the personality, day after day I continue to manage the complexities of my life.

Thank God my loved ones and true friends remain despite the struggles to love myself. With all of me I thank you. We believe in God and have faith that this insanity will be unraveled. One day at a time, sweet Jesus, is all I am asking of You.

Well, like this writing, I am at the end of the storm. The last remaining clouds are passing over. The sunshine is peaking through, and I have survived to fight another day. Now in my clarity I remember something I once read, it went something like this, "That when the past quarrels with the present there can be no future." These words bring me inspiration of hope to let go and move on. Not all is sad because with each battle I learn of a new weapon to add to my arsenal, today this pen has wielded a sword, defeating a worthy opponent.

Depression will surely rear its ugly head again in my life. But when I see it on the horizon of my mind, I will sound the battle cry. With pen and paper in hand I will stand upon already conquered ground.

Brandon Davila

Grateful and Blessed

I'm grateful for when she answers the phone and decides to press 5 and bless me with 30 minutes of her time and when I go to say goodbye she tells me to call right back, yeah man, I'm grateful and blessed for that.

I'm grateful for a shot at a second chance, lookin' back on the last 12 past and how these last 3 can't pass fast enough, and yes it's been rough, but never once have I thought about givin' up. 180 months some say was too much, and just how tough it's been on my loved ones I'll never really know, so I'm grateful and blessed for their love because without it I'll never have grown.

I'm grateful for Sunday mornin' visits and how my mom awakes before the crickets greetin' the same moon she went to sleep with, avoidin' speedin' tickets on her way to the prison. She deserves a ribbon for world's greatest mother. Her love is the 8th wonder and I wonder what I did to deserve such a parent. Her love and support I cherish, and I hope and pray my children inherit her heart, soul, and work ethic. I'm grateful and blessed for my mother's protection.

I'm grateful for knowin' what true love feels like. At night prayin' to God to keep you and the family alright, quickly fallin' asleep dreamin' about your eyes. The same eyes that give me butterflies and have my heart burstin' at the seams everytime I see the girl of my dreams, and it seems that this love will continue to grow, so I'm grateful and blessed for whatever tomorrow holds.

I'm grateful for real friendships and the ups and downs that come with it. Pictures of the kids sent along with a card filled full of birthday wishes, hugs and kisses beside the promise to come and visit. They get what I need to get through and when we talk it's like we are in the same room, for that I'm grateful and blessed to have a friend in you.

I'm grateful for forgiveness and my education, for your patience and each new day.

I'm blessed to be loved and missed, teased with a kiss, and how to love in a whole new way.

I'm grateful for each tear, rain drop, and grey sky, so I'm blessed for each smile, ray of sunshine, and a whole 'nother million reasons why.

I see just as much beauty in the light as I do the dark.

I see the beauty in each soul and the love in every heart.

I am grateful.

I am blessed.

Francisco Hernandez

Gratitude

What do I feel in my life?
I feel the blessings of God poured over me,
him finding a way to fill my heart.
He is a light that lights my path.

What do I see?
I see my grandchildren learning to crawl,
taking their first steps, running.
I see my family enjoying a late summer evening
around a table of food
under a big oak tree.
Hummingbirds bouncing from
bright yellow colored flowers, to deep red poppies,
nectar flowing from an endless well.
I see my wife in her white dress,
the sun reflecting off the lake
sending light in all directions,
light catching in her hair, letting her glow.

What do I hear?
I hear the laughter of the children dancing.
I hear my mother's voice vibrate through my chest.
I hear the voice inside me saying,
this is my purpose, this is my meaning, this gives me strength.
This is what lets me live,
hope unwavering.

Francisco Hernandez

Tanager

Phillip

Over the Years

I just want to say thanks for all you've done to help me over the years. Well, I don't just want to say thanks; I want to say a lot but I won't. I know that over the years, I wasn't always an easy person to deal with, and yet you still helped me, and I thank you for that.

I want to thank you for so many things. You and I already know what you've done for me; yes, I've thanked you before but what you recently helped me with was...my freedom and I will never be able to thank you enough.

You have definitely been an inspiration and role model for me, and because of that I try to imitate the kindness and patience you've given me when I interact with others, which reminds me of a verse in the Bible: "Beloved one, do not imitate what is bad, but imitate what is good. The one who does good originates with God. The one who does bad has not seen God" (3 John 11).

I want to thank you for not judging me, because if you did, I would never be helped. Also, I want to thank you so much for the letters that you've written for me and the invaluable advice. There are no words or enough ways to thank you. I cannot fully express what I feel for what you've done for me.

I just hope that there is someone like yourself for you to go to when you need someone. If ever I can help you, let me know, I'm forever in your debt. I want to let you know how much it meant to me that you've taken the time to help me, over the years. Maybe, things understood don't need to be explained.

Nestor Diaz-Miller

Thankful

It really is a strange feeling not knowing how to be thankful until this present day. At what point in your life is one supposed to learn gratitude? To be grateful for something full-heartedly is a feeling that comes along ever so slowly, or is it taught? Maybe it just is and always will be a part of your life.

For most of my life, I was somewhat of a selfish person. I was only focused on what people could do for me, not ever really interested in how I could help someone else. I believe that being thankful, and I mean being truly thankful, comes from within. It is a stir of emotions. Many times in life we say thank you, but it is of a superficial type rather than a sincere gesture of appreciation.

My great grandfather used to say that he was thankful to be looking down at the ground instead of up towards it. In other words, he was thankful to be alive. I now honestly believe I know how to be thankful. I don't take anything for granted any longer. It has taken me losing almost everything to realize how precious life can really be.

The past several years I have lived in a place where most things in life have been taken away. A place where even the little things can make an incredible difference. Spending quality time with family and sharing a meal or a tender kiss from a sweet someone special. A letter in the mail from someone, anyone. Maybe a phone call to feel somewhat involved.

Having food that tastes like food. Having hot and cold water all the time. Having those small seemingly, irrelevant commodities that help me to fight the good fight. To continue to grasp on to the slight sliver of hope that will get me through one more day.

I am thankful to be where I am at in life. For without being where I am today, the reawakening of my mind would have never happened. I am thankful for my family and friends who truly care about me. They are the reason I can keep on going. They inspire me to be great one day.

I am grateful for being alive.

Francisco Hernandez

Through the Bars

Through the bars
I look at the trees
So full of life
On the other side of the universe
They dance, wave and sing

Birds chirping, trying to tell me
Life goes on
Air catching feathers giving lift

The seasons change
With them I learn
To find fulfillment in what is close
What is around me
What is in me is Divine
Freedom is within

Francisco Hernandez

Cardinal at Rest

We Don't Believe in That

It has always seemed like I was living a contradiction. My core values and morals were constantly being put up against the secular reality of the world, and most times, I didn't mind playing in this arena. After a while, the once thick and definite line between the two became faint. Even with 20/20 vision as an eighteen year-old, this line between my beliefs of how to live a good meaningful life and being a pretentious shallow snob for sheer enjoyment disappeared. I found that how I self identified became blurry, far from the clarity that it once was. Now I spend my days reflecting on my life in hopes of pinpointing exactly when uncertainty solidified itself in my life. The first thought takes me to high school.

During a debate in my Senior Inquiry class, my good friend Eli'yah and I were set to go toe to toe with one another, in a debate. Eli'yah, a well spoken, very opinionated person holds a radically different position than me in almost every aspect of life. I'm not always sure how we have managed to maintain our close friendship for as long as we have, being that we are complete opposites. About half of the seniors in the class would be voting for the first time during the November 2004 election, and the first half of our term was created for us to not only explore the presidential election, but also the local election and the ballot measures that were up for a vote. This day the class was going to be debating the most controversial ballot measures, which consisted of same-sex marriage, property taxes, religion being taught in public school, and abortion rights.

Initially I planned not to be too involved in any of these debates, and only participate in my assigned topic. Arguing points that tend to be totally subjective with people that are usually unwilling to be open up to a different point of view didn't appease me. Eli'yah's assigned topic was one of religion. It was everything that I expected it to be, well developed, super organized, and supported by facts. All was good until he spat out, "Catholics worship Mary and therefore they are disobedient of the word of the Bible!" I snapped into the conversation as if coming back from the dead. What he said was a false statement and I made him aware of this, but according to him his statement was absolutely true. At that point we went from one controversial heated argument to the next. Eventually, he was arguing the pro-life side, and me, the pro-choice side of abortion. This ended with me asserting that, "people should have the freedom to do as they wish, with their bodies, and without regulations" and "A fetus isn't even a person yet!"

After I had arrived at home, there was no one home yet for me to vent about the events that took place earlier in the day. Finally, my mom came home from work and barely got her coat off before I began telling her about Eli'yah's outrageous comments. She was on board with me about the religious part of my narrative, but once I began explaining the abortion rights issues, I was alone and deserted. She waited for me to finish and then softly but sternly said, "SP, we don't believe in that! Let me make myself clear. We don't believe in abortion!" I replied with a simple, "OK."

Although I knew that this was not the stance that I was brought up to take, I had taken it because it is instinctive for me to take the side of the underdog, no matter what the position. I just can't stand a bully who can out talk, out speak, and eventually overrule the timid. My mom pointed out a really poignant issue to me. Sometimes

I compromise my personal beliefs for the sake of others, even when "the others" exist only hypothetically. This habit inevitably skewed the distinction between what I truly believed and the false beliefs that often fled from my mouth. Ultimately, I was put in a real-life circumstance that brought that day of class with Eli'yah to the forefront of my mind.

On an early Tuesday morning I found myself in the cafeteria of the Good Samaritan Legacy hospital, a place that was very familiar to me. My friend Antonio was often hospitalized here to treat his sickle cell anemia attacks. I have spent many days here trying to comfort my friend, but on this morning he is not a patient. He is not the reason why I am in this hospital. I was actually at a clinic just a block away that did not have a place to buy food, so I came to the hospital. I was actually at the nearby clinic with another friend.

Earlier my friend Hannah called me to talk her through a conundrum that she was in. Here she was twenty-years young, living with both of her parents, jobless, single, and pregnant. She called me for support. She was split on what to do. Fifty percent of her wanted to carry out this pregnancy and fifty percent of her wanted to terminate it, and I was elected to be the deciding vote. I had no words to say. I knew what I should say and I also knew what she wanted me to say. Instead of being a stand up man and standing by my convictions, I straddled the fence, and chose to coward out. I gave the pros and cons of both possible choices, and before I knew it I was down at an abortion clinic. I couldn't distinguish my duties as a friend from my duties to the helpless. I suddenly had more obligations to the constitution than to my morals. When I left the clinic in search of food it wasn't hunger that drove me from that clinic, but sheer guilt. Here my friend was upstairs getting God knows what done to her, and I'm chillin' in an ala cart line like all of this was okay. "SP, we don't believe in abortion" is all that kept playing in my head.

As I was headed out of the hospital, Hannah called me on the phone to ask me where I was. She was walking my way. I'm not familiar with abortion procedures, but it had seemed to me that she was done a little too soon. I walk outside towards her. Looking curiously at her, I asked if she was done. Thankfully she didn't go through with the procedure. I was relieved for both her and the unborn fetus but felt disgusted with myself. I like to think that the stress of knowing I was soon going to prison for five years was what clouded my judgment, but now, as I write this from my prison cell, the fact that I passively endorsed the death of one being after I caused the fatality of another makes me feel like a real piece of shit.

Benjamin James Hall

Who Am I

Am I who they say,
a number without a name?
Who simply cannot change,
an item in the lost and found.
Never again to be claimed,
only myself to blame.
Am I what they tell me?

One who feels hands of hate,
trying to choke out all compassion.
Like a dolphin jerked from the safety of water,
into suffocating nets that strangle his vitality.
Like a flightless bird shut in,
its colorful feathers growing dull.

Or am I who I know myself to be,
ever changing and cultivating?
One who thirsts for human touch, a hand of kindness,
a prisoner yes, but a prisoner of hope.

I close my eyes, and my heart soars high,
high above these walls, which is my reality
But never my truth.
Am I who they say?
What they say?
I am free.

Hopes and Dreams

Charles C. Hammond II

Future Encounter

I stumble down the few steps just past the foreboding wall surrounding my confinement that exists between me and my freedom with nervous anticipation of what the future may hold. Many familiar faces run towards me, eager for the first embrace decades after these looming, grey walls initially separated us from one another. Overwhelmed by the sheer beauty of sweet freedom, my heart and mind melds as one and swims off into the distance as if in a dream.

Memories of what used to be no longer align with what now exists. The walkway to the car becomes a birth canal for my reemergence into a society that has long since forgotten its wayward son. I have now become the prodigal son returning from exile.

All seems a blur until the sweet voices of those that ushered me through these many long years without fail bring my feet back to the earth for that long awaited moment in their arms. A mother holding her son once again, free from the bonds of a lifetime ago. A proud father embracing a son that left just a boy, now standing before him a man ready to conquer what awaits. Two sisters regaining a brother lost in battles waged beyond their grasp and ability to overcome. No longer seeing the tattered, lost, and prideful black sheep, but a strong, confident, and changed man seeking to once again be embraced as one of their own. A fractured soul resurrected like a phoenix from the ashes, bright and eager to fly once again among the living. What an encounter that shall be!

Charles C. Hammond II

The Doorway to Nowhere

As I walk these dark and dank hallways, I seek for that one and only doorway that shall release me from the chains that bind me to this place. As a lost apparition seeking the one who could see and hear me as I scream and yell at the top of my lungs for just the slightest recognition, I roam without direction or response. Each doorway that I come to seems to be just beyond my grasp, displacing just enough as I reach for it that the tips of my fingers graze inches from the grasp that I need to turn the knob, to be free at last. All there is to do is to go on to the next, then to the next, and to the next.

As the light begins to fade, I panic and begin to span the chasm that separates me from that fateful doorway to wherever it may lead as long as it's no longer in these hallways that seem to linger for an eternity, but alas my efforts are for not. As in a dream, the hallways stretch before my eyes and the doorways fade to black.

Finally, after 20 years of searching, yearning and reaching I found the one doorway that has not faded. Cautiously I approach, expecting it to flee my grasp; instead, I find my hand around this final doorknob. The knob was cold and hard in my hand, yet turned with ease as if something beckoned me to come. With excitement, I turned the knob and pulled with all of my might. The door was solid oak, heavy, and aged by years of neglect. Slowly it creaks and snaps causing the rusted hinges to buckle and cast off dust, yet it moves. Elated, I pull harder, causing every muscle that I have to strain and burn. It's moving, it's really moving! Through the dust falling and the cobwebs snapping from years of disregard, light shines through and a plume of rancid air, old and stale with a hint of something rotting in the distance blasts past me. Not knowing what to expect I pull all the more in anticipation of what's to come. Sweat across my brow, muscles aching from the strain, it opens to a point that I can now see what's there. Is it freedom, is it family, or is it my demise? I look up in fear of what I might see, but knowing after all this time, I must. Now fully ajar, I see that it leads to another hallway, long, and poorly lit leading to other doorways in the darkness. I now know it was just another doorway to nowhere. Regardless, I begin again in search of the doorway that I seek. Some day, I shall find what I am looking for, but not today. Not today.

HJ Walker

Criminals and Teddy Bears

It may be the most peculiar wonder one could have the chance to observe. Out of place in a world of concrete, iron bars, guard towers, tattooed criminals, gang members, murderers and thieves. Men from all walks of life, from every ethnic group and religious background carrying around stuffed animals in a maximum security prison.

White gorillas, pink monkeys, brown giraffes dressed in baby clothes. Each put in a baby carrier and carried around their necks. It is an amazing sight to behold. Could this be the eighth wonder of the world? The program is called Parenting Inside and Out. Men who have been deemed by society to be misfits and incorrigible are lining up to take this course.

Rival gang members, inmates who would never normally associate with each other are rubbing elbows. The tension is so thick you can see it pour out of their tattooed bodies, as they view each other with eyes of suspicion darting back and forth. But as wax melts when exposed to heat, hardened hearts crumble to the material of the class. Their tough guy exteriors swept out to sea, before the tidal wave of childhood emotions. Memories, love for their children melts even the most hardened.

Watching the masks behind the billboard of faces be removed was to witness a miracle. The transformation was absolutely amazing. In a simple three-month course, these hardened criminals, gang bangers, and murderers were no longer squaring off with antiquated mentalities. Now, they were building futures together for their children, instead of only dreaming for themselves. Exercises in role-playing taught them to play together like their children were doing in the visiting room. Nurturing their own lost child back to health by learning a new language of love.

Many programs have been introduced to prison populations in an attempt to rehabilitate and curb the recidivism rate. None can accomplish this like the love for a child, whether it is the child without or within. Teddy bears behind guard towers can transform one heart at time. The generational cycle of incarceration can be broken.

HJ Walker

Discovery of Self

The child that enters life is molded and shaped how they are to see themselves and the world as a whole.

I am sure the dreams of my parents were not for me to spend a lifetime of incarceration, struggling with self doubt and addictive behaviors. I imagine they have asked the questions what happened, where did we go so wrong, at least a thousand times? Or maybe they came to the conclusion that it was impossible to find the source, to lay the blame at anyone's feet.

Growing up I may have been like all other kids on the outside, but the way I saw myself and the world was cruel. While the other kids were investigating the world around them, I was busy trying to hide in the shadows. My dreams and desires were buried in self loathing. My curiosity of how life worked was clothed in fears of rejection and defeat.

Not all my memories are filled with darkness. The more I investigate I am able to find pieces of a happy child. I loved the red skateboard I received one Christmas. It allowed me to be a part of my older brother's life, as I would ride it up and down the sidewalk, he and his friends popped wheelies on their bicycles. I found great pleasure going on family outings to the ocean. My dad would load up the station wagon with us kids, a cooler full of sandwiches, soda pops and chips, precious memories of times that my father's touches were not in disapproval.

Not until much later in life did I begin to realize that my family wasn't normal. Don't get me wrong, I love all of them and wouldn't trade any of them in for the world, but a fact is a fact; my family was gravely ill. Alcohol and drug addictions, mental and sexual abuse, and criminality ran rampant in the household. The teachings of family values were at the end of leather belts, tree limbs or extension cords, leaving bruises and angry welts on the legs, the lower back and buttocks. Made to feel shameful for who I was through the language of violence. Unworthy, for the little bastard will never amount to anything is the way I understood their love language. It was a young mind at the mercy of generational dysfunctions. Out of nine children all have seen the inside of jail cells, addicted in one form or another to drugs and alcohol, and trapped in abusive relationships.

When I first entered the justice system it only reaffirmed my family's values of worthlessness. State psychologist said, "He's unredeemable, no reason to waste time and resources with this one, lock him up and throw away the key." I am not blaming anyone, nor am I holding any resentment. Today, I am responsible for myself and thank God I have enough sanity to understand, but back then I was only a child!

I have sat in jails, and institutions growing old. Like I imagine my parents must have done, I have asked the proverbial question, what the hell happened? For years I have tried to answer this question that was proving to be very evasive. I found the question too hard to unscramble amidst the bombardment of self doubt and condemnation. I was ready to concede to the belief that clarity was too intangible to grasp. It was at this time of despair that the faintest of light flickered, and I grabbed hold.

Things I should have learned as a child I am now understanding in my elder years, which just goes to show you that psychology is an inexact science, and old dogs can learn new tricks. The key I have found is simply education. Not necessarily wooden desks, school books, classrooms and college professors, but education that is found in the discovery that I am of value and the world isn't this fearful place. Education that has been found in a terminology called Restorative Justice, a place of acceptance and forgiveness. A new world has opened up before my eyes. A journey of childhood curiosities long dead has been born again. Hopes and dreams blossoming, no longer willing to be defined by outside influences. Education has broken the chains of restraint and given me a clear pathway to talents that have been buried within far too long.

Brandon Davila

Dream

Never will I allow a day to go by without me tellin' you a million times that I love you. And we both know it's the little things in life, but still I will spoil you. I will take the dog out without havin' to be asked, even the trash too. Dinner's on me tonight, no fast food. I'll get up in the kitchen and whip us up somethin' delicious and when we are done I'll even do the dishes.

A thousand and one wishes I am forever at your command, and as long as you are my girl I will forever be your man. I want to hold hands when we walk and steal kisses every chance that I get, I want to sit and listen or just kick it, I want to put the world in your hands even if it's too big to fit.

This dream is all I need because it's all I've ever had. Never will I allow a night to go by without you fallin' asleep in my arms, your hair ticklin' my nose, nor will I rest until the whole world knows that as far as love goes, mine grows for you with no end in sight. My life is dull without the light of your gentle touch and everyday plus eternity will never be enough. Our love is what fairy tales are made of and when I wake up….

This will no longer be a dream, but the reality that I have longed for. Rollin' outta bed trippin' over the toys on the floor, lookin' at you as you snore, at peace in your dreams about Channing Tatum. I close the door as our baby girl complains about her brother and how much she hates him. I smile and she gives me a weird look, one that she definitely got from you. I ask what she wants for breakfast and she just storms off. As I enter the kitchen our baby boy is eatin' cereal, the whole box, my cocoa crispies, and yes he gets that from me. You walk in half asleep in some sweats and one of my tees, hair gone crazy, and at that moment you are the most beautiful woman that I have ever seen. This dream is all I will ever need!

Brandon Davila

Dream Big!!!

As a kid nobody was cooler than Superman. I used to dream about flyin' and savin' helpless girls. Then one night Superman was comin' on TV and my mom brought my mattress out into the living room so that I could watch Clark Kent in action as I fell asleep. My mom goes into the kitchen to whip up some Jiffy Pop and I decide it is time to make my dream a reality. I tuck my little blanket into the back of my shirt; I got my cape on tight. I get to jumpin' on my mattress knowing that the next bounce will send me into flight. My mom yells at me to stop jumpin' on the bed. I don't choose to listen because the next jump will send me soarin', leapin' tall buildings in a single bound! NOPE! The next jump sent me face first into the fireplace. I remember the doctors trying to pin me down as they stitched my face back together. When I go to the doctor to get my stitches taken out the nurse has the balls to give me a damn Superman sticker. Screw Superman!!! I mean for real. Who wants to be Superman? The dude wears his drawers on the outside of his tights. I dream of better things. Bigger things. You will never fly, it is impossible; no matter how hard you try. No, not me, what I dream of becoming is way more real…a Ninja Turtle!

SP

Emotional Garbage

I wait to write because nowhere seems to be the right spot. Fear of someone reading my vulnerability keeps me from writing altogether, but thankfully it is Wednesday. Anxiously, I want to bolt from my transitional renters' class to my safe haven, so I can finally vomit pent-up emotional garbage that has been weighing me down.

I feel like the faded black pants of the officers whose purpose is to be washed, worn, and witness the day-to-day dysfunction of many facets. Today, and hopefully only today, I feel like the ugly tan and dull brown colors that taunt me at every turn. Forever ugly and forever trapped.

Today, I feel like the flip side of my journey to prison. Yes, I know my experience but never knew my friend's; the uncertainty, the sudden change that occurs, not giving you the option to opt out. "Today I am your friend, next week, next month, next year; I may just be a memory", are the words of Terrance that pull on me harder than the gravitational pull of a black hole. Him, afraid he would keep his end of the bargain and that I'd breach mine. Now I only understand all too well what he was going through.

This dismal mood continues, but, Robyn tells me, "You have to put your head back on and get yourself together. All will get better when this hurt is gone." She encourages me to find that indestructible fight that I miss so much from within myself. I just wish I could pinpoint the hurt I was going through. Self-doubt? Inadequacy? No! Being, or at least feeling, like I am a shell of myself has been the most difficult to reconcile. Everything about my existence feels theoretical, nothing is certain. I'm stuck in a DeLorean that has failed to move. Emotionally, mentally and physically, I have remained in 2008 for the past five years. The propulsion that experiences give to growth has ceased. Who am I? Who will I be? What have I become? I have not a clue and that ignorance jabs and possesses my self-talk, turning it from cheery to dreary.

Theoretically I will be a student, then an engineer, but what if I am not good enough? My Achilles heel, not being good enough. The only thing that is certain is that I will be a son, a brother, and a felon with big dreams. Negative self-talk creeps in.

Today, I feel hopeful because having hope means there is a possibility and something to look forward to, to work towards. Today, I will muster up at least a slice of the self-esteem of my former self.

Benjamin James Hall

Hope's Highway

Her voice from the bedroom pulls him away from the mundane.
Her soft, quiet tone is the soundtrack to his life.
Her eyes are lighthouses shimmering off the water,
With transformative power.
A lifeboat for the darker times past.

Windows to her soul and the blood rushing to her cheeks,
Reveal the news without another vocal syllable spoken.
His whole body smiles looking at her.
The radio dial in his soul, tuned to joy's station
With undistorted clarity.
He could almost remove tomorrow from his mind,
Making a lifetime of this moment.
But tomorrow holds such bliss.

Only God could have brought this woman into his life.
For he knows her love must be supernatural.
To wait for him, looking past his shipwrecked selfish existence,
And seeing God's purpose in him, becoming his bride.

He cannot speak, gratitude overpowering his emotions,
Running his fingers through her hair,
Lifting her shirt, pressing his ear against her navel,
Listening to the now two hearts inside.

Droplets of salty ecstasy trickle from his banjo eyes,
Splashing her skin.
He is a man who never need fly anywhere for vacation.
For here is the most exotic locale he will ever know,
This side of eternity.

He can hear the rustling of sack lunches outside his window,
Bells and yelling as Corrections Officers feed C-block,
The prison is on lockdown in the wake of racial violence.
Reality pulls him back from the highways he was just wandering.
Where the road signs all read Hope.

The prisoner sits alone,
Selfishly hoping the lockdown will last a little longer.
Captive yet free,
Sorrowful, and yet joyful.
The prisoner wishes, he imagines, he desires.
The convict hopes and dreams,
spilling his ink with tears onto the page

Francisco Hernandez

Mercy

The headline reads "College for Convicts Instead of K-12 Education." Sometime ago this headline could have read "College for Blacks Instead of White Students," or "Jobs for Women Instead of Men." Talking points and slogans are so often used to instill fear and make dividing lines that are black and white, hate or acceptance. What is the result when these kinds of attitudes prevail? This is the kind of speech that has created groups that are seen as second-class citizens. For incarcerated people, two things are stripped away: our freedom and our humanity. The loss of our freedom is logical; what is not logical is that there are people who see us and other groups as having no human worth, right to equality, or mercy. Furthermore, those who speak out against this kind of oppressive thinking are often shown scorn. They are hated, attacked, and even murdered.

How do retribution and revenge make our lives and society any better? Does that not just keep the cycle of inequality, racism, and injustice going? Who are the ones who show a different way? How do we all learn mercy? Why are the poor treated so unfairly? Bryan Stevenson says, "We live in a society that treats the rich and guilty more fairly than the poor and innocent." What are the factors that have led to this?

The mentality of the previously mentioned headline explains some for where we are, "College for Convicts Instead of K-12 Education." The headline implies that convicts are taking all education from K-12. Common sense tells us that this is not true, yet there it is, just more politics of hate and fear. Being a father of two boys who went to public schools, I believe that K-12 education is very important. Everyone else does, too, and public schools here in Oregon receive more than 7 billion dollars per biennium. Shouldn't safe communities for all citizens be a priority, too? Educating the incarcerated dramatically reduces that person's chance to recidivate. It costs less than $9,000 to give an incarcerated person a two-year degree, and a lifetime of well-being, while it costs the state $31,000 a year to incarcerate me. Any person who intelligently considers this would see that education is an excellent investment in money and in the external benefits that cannot be measured in money.

But there has always been a lack of intelligence when people engage in stereotypes, prejudice, and discrimination. Ignorance most often is precisely what drives these mentalities. We need more leaders who look at the bigger picture and strike a balance that creates the most benefits for all. We need opportunity that leads to redemption, not repression that leads to resentment.

Why do those who speak out against injustices often end up paying such a high price? Like the Rev. Martin Luther King Jr., Cesar Chavez, President Abraham Lincoln, or Dietrich Bonhoeffer who was executed in a concentration camp for speaking out against Hitler and the Nazi's injustice and genocide. It seems that people will go to the extreme to feel better than, to have a finger to point at. At the time, those who oppressed vehemently believed that what they were doing was right. But history has shown that they were wrong in morals, ethics, and actions.

When people spoke out against slavery they were treated as traitors. Called un-American, they were hated and reviled; some were even murdered for their strong belief that all people deserve freedom and dignity. Yet in the face of these great persecutions they prevailed, and hope was won for a great multitude of people. The 13th Amendment to the Constitution of the United States of America freed the slaves, but it left one exemption, those who are incarcerated. The 13th Amendment reads, "Neither slavery nor involuntary servitude, except as a punishment for a crime whereof the party shall have been duly convicted, shall exist in the United States or any place subject to their jurisdiction." Those who are incarcerated can still be used as slave labor. At the end of the Civil War our country incarcerated large numbers of freed African Americans and used them as a labor force to create large economic profits, as still happens today. These people were often given lengthy prison sentences for petty crimes. They lived in deplorable conditions and many died of mistreatment.

How does this apply to today? The 13th Amendment left the door open for a group of people to continue to be treated as property, or animals like cattle, just as in the time of slavery. Even so, it is not the abuse of human beings through forced labor that is the gravest of injustices. It is the concept that we have a group of people that are looked at and treated as untouchables, as having less value, as maybe not being human. It makes it much easier on the conscience when one mistreats something viewed as slightly less than human. If not human then why do they deserve a job, education, a place to live, dignity, empathy, mercy, compassion, and justice? It is this mentality that prevails in our media and society in general. This injustice that formerly incarcerated and incarcerated people face today is similar in some ways to the injustice faced by blacks during the Jim Crow era, the denial of women's rights, and the discriminatory labor practices against Latinos by large farming corporations; the list could go on and on.

Self-righteousness and the inability to understand the context of others and situations is what has led to the ignorant thinking that has permeated our society in regard to discrimination and intolerance. In the Bible there is a story of the self-righteous Teachers of the Law and the Pharisees who bring a woman caught in adultery to Jesus to have her stoned. Jesus says nothing, bends down, and writes something in the ground. Then he says, "If any of you is without sin let him be the first to throw the first stone at her" (John 8:7). Again he bent down and wrote something in the ground. Finally, no one could throw a stone, so they all walked away. Jesus didn't condemn the woman but showed mercy and told her to sin no more. What did Jesus write in the ground, what could Jesus write about me and every person on this earth? Jesus knows that we all have done wrong, but he understands grace and mercy, too.

What was the context of this woman's life? What kind of emotional, mental, and physical scars did she carry? What kind of pain and wounds do those who are incarcerated carry? Speaking from my experience and others I've talked to, a large number of us were children who grew up with alcoholic and/or drug addicted parents, in homes where they were physically, mentally, emotionally, or sexually abused or even tortured, where there were unspeakable things done to them. Some grew up in foster homes and in the streets because they did not have stable homes. Some were not shown love, compassion, or empathy. Many of them were broken and never really given a chance. Some would say that we all have a choice, and in some ways that is true, but when you take a person who has experienced such hurt and damage, it becomes difficult to break this cycle. But when mercy and opportunity are given, people can change. I have been the chief of sinners, yet here I am in front of you a new man. Transformed from the broken person I was into a man with hope and a purpose.

When people are shown mercy they are given a second chance in which great things can be achieved. King David, Moses, and the Apostle Paul all committed murder, yet their accomplishments when given the chance were staggering. Paul helped spread the gospel that has literally touched the lives of billions of people. What drove him to this? It was the mercy shown to him by Jesus on the road to Damascus as he went about his persecution. It was there he saw a light that changed his life forever. My hope is that all those who have not seen this light will some day see it and learn what mercy is and therefore be able to give it.

The hateful headline, "College for Convicts Instead of K-12 Education," does nothing to make the lives of our families any better. It does nothing to bring about dignity for the human spirit or right the injustices of our present and past. The benefit this kind of speech brings for the few does not justify the damage it does to the millions. My brothers and sisters, let's wake up and light the torch of justice and mercy. Let's demand that our elected officials and people in positions of power no longer engage in politics of discrimination that are meant to degrade human beings. Leaders like the Rev. Martin Luther King Jr. have brought us this far in our fight, let's take it to the finish line and see our dream come true of extinguishing hate. Let's be the example.

Francisco Hernandez

My Window

As I look out my window the bars obstruct my view, but looking past the confinement in the distance I see the migrating Canadian geese traveling south from their home in the north, flying in V-formation with the red fall sky painted as a backdrop behind them. It's that time of year again, another year of time and space gone by like a blob of uncomprehending mess. The geese will leave us with their mess, goose shit everywhere, and this fact reminds me that it's fall again. Another year gone by has left me trying to look back at the frames in my mind, to find the gems of life in the mist of time.

My soul longs to live. I want to live life, to feel the embrace of the lady in white, whose skin is like silk radiating the light. But all I hear is "Do not touch what you cannot have. These are human feelings and you are animal, devoid of human life. Beast." I am labeled a freak.

I want to live life. I want to shout and run in the mist between the trees, to climb the mountains that dance around in my dreams. I want to dance to the loud music I feel in my inner chest and feel the joy rush in the air between myself and them.

The bars obstruct my view. I can't see or do these things, so I settle to living life halfway, to feeling halfway, touching halfway, and being human halfway. This is my life, a half-life, a half mind, a half-man. My window.

Francisco Hernandez

Winter Swan

Phillip

Patience

Sitting across, Dark hair
Unblinking, she stares
She whispers something, I cannot hear
She points at something, far or near

I reach across, she pulls away
Did I scare her, what can I say

Can't remember how long it's been
Can't wait to see Peychence again

Phillip

Exit Interview

I have done twenty-six plus years in prison. Needless to say, prison has been a big part of my life. In 2011 I went before the parole board for an exit interview to be released. I got flopped two years; in other words, I didn't get released, and I got deferred two years. At the time I felt that I was ready to be released, however the parole board felt I wasn't. Now looking back I agree that I wasn't ready to be released. I can handle the time; what I couldn't handle was the phone call I had to make to my family to let them know that I wasn't getting out for at least two more years. I don't know if you have ever heard your mother cry. I have and it wasn't something I ever want to hear again. When I heard my mother cry because I wasn't getting out, because of the decisions I've made in my life, knowing that I made her cry, let me tell you that is not a good feeling to have or hear. I felt so bad and ashamed of myself. I can't even imagine how she felt.

I took to heart the parole board's decision and for the next two years, I took as many programs as I could handle to better myself and become a better person. I took Anger Management twice, Addictive Mindset, NA/AA, 33 week Crime Sharing Group, Gender Awareness, Empathy Class, Dialogue Class, Transition classes, and graduated with a Chemeketa Community College degree, not to mention Parenting Inside-Out, and Parenting Aide for six months, while working three jobs and only getting paid for one!

In August 2013, I received a letter from the board letting me know that I have to take a psych test before my hearing. A month later I am notified that they request a second psych test. If you've never taken a psych test before, the only way I can describe it it's like being naked in front of a stranger that holds your mental being in their cold sterile hands. When you see them and talk to them, you have to be totally honest. If I had to sum it up in one word, it would be "Submit" because any other way will only hurt later and they know if you are BS-ing them.

December 2013 is my hearing and it is quickly approaching. I feel I have enough time to put together my parole plans when I get a letter from the parole board telling me that I am scheduled to see them in November 2013 instead of December 2013. Now I'm feeling rushed because I am a month behind. What the...? A few weeks later I received another letter saying that I am now going to see them in December instead of November; I don't know how to take that news. Should I look at it as a bad sign or what? This usually doesn't happen, for them to change it.

As fate would have it, it was a blessing in disguise. It gave me an extra month to prepare for my hearing, and I truly needed it because I thought I was ready but I wasn't. The morning of my hearing I am waiting in my cell to be called to the board. I don't feel nervous; I actually feel calm with a touch of butterflies but not nervous, hmm.

I'm in my cell when they do call me. I walk to receiving and discharge, where they ask me my name and state identification number, and then they have me wait in the holding cell for about 15 minutes. Then an officer comes in with leg shackles and belly chains, pats me down and puts the chains on me.

Two officers escort me to the Superintendent's office for my hearing. We get to the foyer area and they have me wait there for about 10 minutes because the board isn't ready yet. All these stops haven't stressed me out, yet. Let me say this, I did a lot of praying to God and put whatever decision that was going to happen in His hands and accept whatever happened to me because I have no control of the future.

I spent close to two hours in my hearing, advocating for my release, reminding the board over and over what I have done to better myself and what I have learned to turn my life around. For the last two years I have not wasted my time doing nothing, that I have been programming, rehabilitating myself, the person that they are talking about was a person from the past, twenty-six years ago. The person before them is not that person that they are talking about anymore. The hearing is over, and they have me leave the room for deliberation. I'm waiting in the foyer again, this time for them to call me back in to give me my decision. I didn't waste my time sitting in the foyer either; I prayed the entire time I was out there. Fifteen minutes later the clerk comes out and says they are ready for me.

I walk back into the conference room, carefully aware of my leg irons, and notice that no one is looking at me. I immediately have a flashback to my jury trial, no eye contact from the jury meant bad news. I prepared myself for the words "deferred two years." Instead I heard the word "affirmed" and then I noticed the board members all looking at me and one was even smiling. My hearing seemed to escape me. I had tunnel vision in my ears. It sounded like I was in a stadium and someone was talking, but I couldn't hear. I only saw her mouth moving. It was a trip: I think I went into shock. I felt that this day would eventually get here and yet I never expected it. That extra month made all the difference; let me just say that God works in mysterious ways.

It has been a few weeks since I've seen the parole board. I get a grip to gather my thoughts on returning back to civilization and also play back the hearing in my head and what they said to me. It comes back to me in increments, but not in order.

Now I am looking in the paper for clothes to wear for when I am released, it's not that easy when you don't really know what size you wear. I've been staying away from bright colors. I picked out a pair of black jeans and a dark green T-shirt. I can't even picture myself wearing anything other than blue jeans and a blue T-shirt.

It's not that easy to just change gears and your lifestyle behind bars for over two decades but I'll eventually adjust. I am paroling to a half-way house in Portland instead of going back home. I feel that I need to slowly integrate back into the community and not disrupt my family's way of life on my account. Eventually I'll go home. While I am on active parole I plan on enrolling at Portland State University and obtain a degree in business, and complete the 300 and 400 series in Spanish, along with a part-time job.

For now this is it, but my story is far from over. To be continued…

Benjamin James Hall

The Moon Through the Bars

Suppose you took a moment away from your busy,
hectic, humdrum life and looked up.
Looked up to admire the heavens
which perhaps you don't remember,
the last time you stopped to consider
and beheld their magnificence.

Suppose you enjoyed what you saw and imagine
you were someplace
where the man-made lights
continually drown out the splendor of the stars
and you rarely saw the moon.

Suppose you had no one to go home to and imagine…
Imagine at this moment someone,
somewhere in the dark, a stranger to you
is looking up at the same sky and trying not to cry.

Supposing I am laying in the dark
yet surrounded by floodlights
and I'm looking up through a small gap
through the window bars where I can see the moon.
Imagine I am thinking about you,
a nameless, faceless stranger.

Wondering if you are admiring the same moon,
wishing I were there next to you.

The soft sound of the sprinkler in the C-block yard,
the quiet hum of the fan on the empty tier,
a simple comfort to me.

Suppose you could look through my eyes,
if only for a moment.
Feel what I feel and touch the hope that is in my heart.
And believe the next time
you fix your eyes upon a star that perhaps...

Perhaps you don't really know,
just how blessed you are.
And conceive from now on,
you won't just hurry on your way
without stopping to breathe in,
breathe in and behold
all the beauty and majesty around you.
Suppose...

Francisco Hernandez

The New Unwanted

How can we build a society that does not need prisons? This is a profound question, but maybe the question should be how do we build a society that cares about all human beings? Throughout our society's history we have treated groups of our fellow human beings as inferior, unintelligent, worthy of enslavement, needing dominance over, and at times, treated worse than animals. These ideologies that lead to discrimination, hate, prejudice, and stereotypes have long term effects and consequences for our society.

Prisons in this country are not the problem, but a symptom of much larger issues that people from all walks of life face. The racism that produces inequality and reduces the successful life chances of minorities is part of the problem. There are consequences for our society, when we create such large numbers of people who are shut out of many areas of our economy. With barriers in place, they have a diminished chance of being able to compete fairly in dominant society, some then turn to the underground economy to make a living. With no other choice our society then uses our racist justice system to condemn and punish them. There is little talk of rehabilitation, restoration, empathy, or forgiveness. Consequently, incarcerated people are worse off in the end than they were in the beginning. Now felons, these minorities will never be able to challenge the status quo of the political elite. They have been silenced forever.

I have been incarcerated for the past 16 years now, but that does not matter; upon my release from prison I will continue to face judgment. This judgment will follow me for the rest of my life. I will face discrimination, prejudice and stereotypes. That's the society we live in, which says, "You do not deserve a job, a place to live, a right to vote, the graciousness of forgiveness, empathy, or value as a human being." Maybe this sounds familiar of past times, or maybe we have always just treated one group or another this way.

I am a third class citizen, a Latino convicted of a crime. We who are convicted of a crime are third class citizens. We are the black men and women of the 1960's in a southern state. We are the women of the 1910's who did not have the right to vote. We are the Mexican of years past who was only good enough for low-paying menial jobs. We are a minority of low resources, a people with no voice. No voting rights equal no voice, how better to keep unwanted people subjugated in a democratic society? It worked for women and minorities for many years, and it will work for the new unwanted of today.

How different would our society be if we believed and acted on the belief that every human being has immense value no matter what the race, color, sex, class, identity, free, or incarcerated? What if we believed that no person can be defined for the rest of their lives by one act? We need to do away with the politics of fear, and embrace reason and understanding when it comes to looking at the incarcerated. One in 33 people in this country are under some form of correctional supervision (in jail, prison, on parole, or probation). These are our sons, daughters, mothers, fathers, husbands and wives, not monsters and beasts.

When will we no longer need prisons? When our society stops singling out people to point the finger at in judgment; until we stop using hate and discrimination to keep the "other" down; until the cycle of inequality is extinguished; and until we all as a society, free or incarcerated, learn to share in humanity. Giving opportunity that leads to redemption is not being soft on crime, it's caring about our communities and making our society a better place for all people.

The Rev. Martin Luther King Jr. had a dream, and I believe that dream is still alive. He fought for equality and human dignity, so that we could see his dream of a society where we all live with mercy and compassion towards each other. He ran the race, he fought the good fight, but now he has passed the torch of human justice to us. History shows that people like you and I can have enormous impact in our society if we give the time to care. Maybe we can reach Rev. Martin Luther King Jr.'s dream through hard work, evaluating our own hearts, empathy and compassion.

Brandon Davila

Today

It is hard for me to vision tomorrow without a glimpse of the past. It's not that I can't let go, it's more like that I refuse to. When I stop hurting and the pain fades that means I have forgotten, that my most vivid memories have faded into some countless shades of gray, and I can't have that. I need those memories because they are proof.

Proof that laughter filled the room, that tears were met with warm hugs and ice cream. That holidays were not about the gifts, but the presents of presence. When tomorrow comes all I will have is the memory, but I am a good story teller, so without a doubt reality will exist.

Today will fade into yesterday and tomorrow will be today, and still I love the same, miss what is gone and blessed for the same. When the stars align and the moon greets the sun, the blurred lines, those of the here and now, and the days past, merge, creating my Eden.

Now when I glimpse into my past, I smile, for my vision of tomorrow blinds. All made possible because I was blessed with today.

Inside

James M. Anderson

Fear, Chains, and Ankle Irons

The stale odor of rusty metal and men in dire need of showers marked my first day in prison. Stepping into an adult prison shocked my sense of smell and made me long for the days of my lavender and rosemary smelling home on Marcel Court. They were odors that time would help me grow accustomed to, but never the ability to grow comfortable with. That first day in prison fifteen years ago was a nightmare. A nightmare that I never thought would end. I was 17 back then, and at that point in my life I'd yet to experience a whisker on the chin, let alone the reality of being surrounded by convicts. Sentenced as an adult, I was sent to the men's prison for one of the roughest wake-up calls that a young man could ever get. The worst part? No one was there to prepare me for how drastically my life was about to change. For the first time in my life, I was completely alone.

That early April morning in 1997 began at McLaren, a youth offender facility located in my hometown of Woodburn, Oregon. It's weird thinking about it now, but thousands of times I must have passed that securely fenced juvenile jail without even giving it a second thought. You see, riding bikes with my friends was a favorite joy of mine, one that I still miss terribly to this day. My friends and I would often pedal along innocently without a care in the world during our summer months of freedom. Summer months heading nowhere and everywhere all at once. Freedom. A word many people fail to understand or appreciate until it's gone in a momentary lapse of judgment.

As we'd pedal past McLaren's fenced-in perimeter I never paid attention to its haunting coldness, or for that matter, to the fact that there were hundreds of juveniles housed within its confines who were stripped of their ability to roam. Juveniles that were just like me; all pimples, awkward knees, and unrefined skills that often led to bad choices. I never gave thought to the idea that beyond my teenage world of unhindered freedom an existence entirely different than my own was not only possible, but waiting just around the corner to welcome me. When I was sentenced to 25 years to life as that awkward kneed, pimply juvenile, McLaren became a quick stepping stone before I was transferred to an adult correctional facility. My stay there was brief, a week, week and a half at most. Soon the dreaded day arrived, though I remember hoping mightily that it never would.

As I awoke that morning dripping in stress induced perspiration and flooded with crippling anxiety, I remember wondering to myself if I'd even make it through the following night. I was yanked out of my dank holding cell around 10:30 a.m. by one of the staff who always seemed to refer to us as "pukes", kids who were more deserving of a bullet than a second chance. "The big day's here," was all he'd said, excitement apparent in his voice. I knew what he meant. The guard whistled the Queen tune "Another One Bites The Dust" as he wheeled in a bucket full of handcuffs, ankle cuffs, and double linked belly chains. I was chained and bound with careful attention to detail, almost as though I were Hannibal Lecter himself. I was mortified. The heaviness of all that metal hanging from my body was something I wasn't prepared for, and it was rigged so tight that taking a deep breath was all but impossible. I stood there quietly, hot tears burning trails of regret down my face, shivering with fear.

Tiny step by tiny step, I was led outside and toward the "Blue

Bird," which was known by all who entered the criminal justice system as the bus that would transport prisoners to one of the state's many adult penitentiaries. I was crying softly as I neared the "Blue Bird". Everything at that moment became so real, and I felt the crushing weight of adulthood wrapping its arms around me tightly and pushing me forcefully toward the bus as I realized Mom could never be there to save me again.

"This one here's sort of a softie, gentlemen," said my escort as he stood in the bus entrance, "who needs a girlfriend?" It was the McLaren guard's parting shot at me, and it was a doozie. A bullet of terror coursed through my veins as I comprehended what being a man's girlfriend in prison entailed.

As I struggled to make my way up the bus's steep steps, I realized 30 of the meanest looking guys I'd ever seen were all staring directly at me. Each of them at least fifteen to twenty years my senior, all of them infinitely more knowledgeable about how to survive in prison. Some laughed, others whistled. All saw me as a potential victim. That much I knew. At 150 pounds, and with the fear of God in my eyes, I suppose I wasn't very intimidating. I tried to hide my tears by tilting my head to the side and brushing my cheeks across my shoulders, but I'm sure it didn't fool them since my face was clearly flushed.

I kept my eyes down. I kept them down because I didn't want to lock eyes with someone who'd mistake it for a challenge and use it against me at a later date. Besides, you never look a wild beast in the eyes. That's what I remember some long forgotten TV show saying anyways, and it was good enough advice for me. I applied it immediately.

I slowly made my way to the rear of the bus where the last seat was open, each convict that I passed sizing me up and down as I walked.

Unfortunately the last seat was next to a horrendously rough looking biker with a ZZ Top beard and a freshly shaven head. He had the smile of a career methamphetamine user, clear blue eyes that seemed to look right through me, and a tattoo that said "mama tried" in faded black ink across the left side of his neck. He was scary. No exaggeration. I thought everyone on the bus, including the armed guards clutching their shotguns tightly, could hear my heart pounding viciously within my teenage chest. I clenched my teeth and fists hoping that by doing so the men around me wouldn't notice how badly I was shaking. I was literally on a one way ride to hell. And I was scared.

During the ride the convicts joked that I looked all of about 14 years old, and when I puffed my chest out and said, "Nope, I'm 17," they roared with laughter and said I was probably getting dropped off at Hillcrest, which is another local youth facility. What they didn't realize was I was in it for the long haul. I was going to "gladiator school", which is what the Oregon State Correctional Institute (OSCI) was known as back then due to the amount of violence its walls contained. I don't know about gladiator, but I definitely could have passed for a scrawny Peter Pan, all of which didn't bode well for me. The one piece of advice that ZZ Top guy gave me was that the first thing a "newbie" needs to do is get a big piece of steel and make an example out of somebody. I think he was trying to scare me, and it worked.

I arrived at OSCI around noon. It was a cold and rainy day, and the windows on the bus were nearly completely fogged over. As we pulled to a stop directly in front of the prison I craned my neck so that I could get a glimpse of my new home. It's not what anyone in their right mind would call home, but seeing the seriousness of the rows and rows of razor wire surrounding the perimeter through the fogged over windows was enough to tell me immediately that it was.

At least until I was allowed to leave, which was still decades down the road and an unfathomable amount of time to try to visualize, I was looking at my home. We slowly exited the bus and stepped single file into a line. I distinctly remember the transport officer yelling loudly that everyone needed to stand closer to the person in front of us. "Nuts to butts" were his exact words. The convicts grew increasingly more agitated. At a snail's pace we made our way toward the prison tiny step by tiny step, the ankle chains digging deeper and deeper into my flesh with each lift of my leg. We were a chain gang. A group of men being led into exile.

After being unshackled I was told to undress and kick my white transport jumpsuit into a pile to my left. Two guards stood within arms' reach of me, canisters of mace the size of small fire extinguishers hanging menacingly at their sides. They barked a list of direct orders; "Let me see in your ears. Run your hands through your hair. Show me your hands. Now flip them over. Lift up your arms and show me your armpits. Lift your penis. Now your balls. Turn around. Lift your foot up. Wiggle your toes. Now the other. Bend over. Spread your cheeks, and give two good coughs. Good." I was then told to stand there quietly until they finished with the others. After awhile, once everyone in the room had given their "two coughs", I was handed prison clothes that were 3 sizes too small and flip flops that were 4 sizes too big. I looked like a carnival clown, and the grin on the prison guards' faces let me know that I was dressed like that solely for their amusement. If you've never been truly embarrassed or insecure, wearing such clothes would quickly sap your self-esteem and reduce you to mockery. Though he didn't come out and say it, I knew this was their way of letting me know that I no longer made my own decisions, not even concerning clothing.

Nope. I was theirs, and I'd go by their rules from now on. Humble pie? Two slices please. As the group strip search finished, the main officer, the big one who looked as though he was specifically chosen for the purpose of intimidation, looked at me and said, "First timer, huh? The boys are gonna love you." The only thing I wanted to do in that moment was scream for my mother. Scream for anyone who would understand that this wasn't the right place for a juvenile, but I knew it was pointless.

The door to the rest of the prison opened and as the other new arrivals and I stepped through, it slammed shut behind us with ear-splitting authority. The type of authority that tells you that comfort is no longer a recognized word. We walked down an incredibly long hallway to the units we were assigned and made our way cautiously down the tiers to our cells as the established convicts eyed us with suspicion. I could tell that we were being looked upon as intruders, unwelcomed guests who could easily be made to disappear.

What I first noticed about cell 264 was how extremely tiny it was. I wondered how two people could possibly live in such a small space without being surgically conjoined. It was smaller than the bathroom that I used at home, and the toilet was within a foot of the bottom bunk. I felt my chest constrict and it took everything I had to force myself into stepping inside. My cellmate was a skinhead in his 40's, an intimidating man who immediately sized me up and down. After deeming me worthy to be in his presence with a simple head nod, he pointed to the top bunk. He had more tattoos than any circus freak I'd ever seen on those late night "Ripley's Believe It or Not" shows, and it took incredible focus in order to not stare in disbelief. He had dozens of nudie mags stacked in various locations throughout the cell, and I didn't know what to say considering I'd only seen those types of magazines behind the counters at Mom and Pop markets. Well, mostly anyways.

After my awkward introduction with my cellmate, I took inventory of my meager prison issued possessions and placed them one by one into my drawer. A plastic comb, a short and pathetic looking plastic toothbrush, a cup of baking soda, two blankets that moths would surely cringe at, and two stain-filled sheets with a rough yet strangely thin pillowcase. After making my bed I remember my cellmate, on the lower bunk eyeball deep in a nudie mag, tossed me a MAD magazine and smirked, "You're not old enough to see these yet anyways youngster." What he failed to understand was that seeing a set of boobs was by far the last thing on my mind. You see, I was busy contemplating the best strategy for survival, or if I'm being completely honest, which method of suicide would be the quickest.

Then, without warning, an insanely loud fire bell screamed to life and went on for what felt like forever. I was ready to stop, drop, and roll! But despite my panic, despite my fear, there was no fire to be found. In actuality, and to my surprise, it was how meals were announced three times a day. This one meant it was dinner time.

"Wow, prison is a nightmare," I remember thinking as I wondered which exact cell Freddy Krueger might be housed in. I mean, surely he was here somewhere, he had to be. It was that scary. I knew things were never going to be normal for me again. Ever.

Dinner? Ha! It looked like a pack of sick dogs all got together and vomited on my dinner tray. I couldn't bring myself to even taste it so I ate one piece of bread and returned reluctantly to cell 264.

I don't remember what hour I fell asleep that first night, but I'm positive it was well after 3 a.m. My nerves, along with my inability to calm down, were like drinking a full pot of coffee and expecting to get a good night's rest, it wasn't going to happen. Not a chance.

"RIIINNGGGGG.....CHOW TIME!" I was jolted awake, that stupid fire bell again. People were yelling loudly, dozens of toilets were flushing all at once, and cell doors were being yanked open and slammed shut with early morning frustrations evident in the slumbered inmates' ferociousness. 5:30 a.m. Breakfast. This was going to take some getting used to, that's for sure. It was the beginning of day number two and as I suspected, life as I had always known it was over. This was my new home for longer than I'd yet to live. Only nine thousand, one hundred and twenty-four more days of hell to go.

HJ Walker

Full Moon

I was tucked away comfortably between my green sheets and gray wool blanket, when the cell door opened with a bang. I was startled, so I turned to see what the commotion was about. There in the doorway was the intimidating figure of a guard, and he was yelling out my name. My heart began to race as he said, "HJ, get dressed and come out here." I calmed down a bit once I got my bearings, realizing that if I was in trouble his handcuffs would be out. Not to mention he would be accompanied by several other officers. In my best effort not to allow my voice to betray the fear in me, I asked, "Am I being requested for work?"

My job title is Crisis Companion, which is a polite way of saying suicidal watch. I have sat in front of cells of individuals who have attempted suicide, and in my opinion belong in the Oregon State Hospital. These are men who paint their cells in their own blood, and their bodies in feces. Who talk to imagined people, and withstand the strongest of antipsychotic drugs. But instead, they are tucked away in a unit here at the Oregon State Penitentiary.

The guard standing at my door responded to my question as to whether I was being requested for work by saying, "I don't know, Control Floor called for you." That was usually news that a crisis was at hand. I had settled in for a night of reality shows, but my time could be better spent than vegetating in front of the television set. Instead, I was in for a night of real life drama live from Oregon's maximum security prison. So I slid my butt out of bed, allowing my feet to hit the cold concrete floor while contemplating not the crisis at hand, but what I would load in my jacket pockets for the long night ahead. I would need a pen and some paper, a book to read in case the individual is sleeping, my Sony transistor radio to drown out the screams, and last but not least a couple candy bars or cookies. I wished my cellie a good night and slid the door shut behind me.

It was past the ten p.m. count so an officer was sent to escort me to the Mental Health building. He was a very talkative individual and eager to explain the crisis at hand. According to him, inmate Mike, (a fictitious name to protect the innocent), received a "Dear John" letter and was having a melt down. "Dear John" being a goodbye letter from a sweetheart. Because Mike appeared to be emotionally unstable he was put on 24 hour suicide watch, even though he never attempted the act itself. I had sat with Mike in the past and believed he was one who belonged in the State Hospital. He was an individual with child-like characteristics who couldn't comprehend reality. Hopefully the psych doctors would have him on some kind of sleeping medication, if not, I was in for a long night of nonsense talking, and not looking forward to it at all.

As Officer Luis (another fictitious name) and I walked on, he was also excitable about an extraction of another inmate from his cell earlier that evening. An extraction usually consists of several guards with shields and mace cans standing in front of your cell, demanding you back up to the bars so they can handcuff you, all the while hoping that you won't. If they have been summoned, their adrenaline is pumping and the air is filled with testosterone. Officer Luis still appeared to be filled with adrenaline as he shared the story.

Inmate Mackey (again another fictitious name) was having a personal crisis with the demons in his head, and causing a ruckus.

Screaming at no one in particular and yelling obscenities. They feared that he was a danger to his cellie, duh. He backed to the bars without incident, which I got the impression from Mr. Luis was disappointing. As they were escorting him to the disciplinary segregation unit, he suddenly plopped down in the middle of the avenue, in the pouring rain and started muttering incoherently. According to Mr. Luis, Mackey was also now in the Mental Health Unit, standing butt naked in a cell talking to himself.

The rain had stopped and the sky was clear. As we walked on and I was listening to Officer Luis' tales I couldn't help but notice there was a full moon, to change the subject I interrupted and said, "Check it out, a full moon." To my surprise Officer Luis got all excited and started to explain how the moon has such a powerful effect upon our planet. How it directly changes the ocean tides and alters the moods of people. You know the saying when people are messing up, "there must be a full moon out." I don't have a clue and said as much, wondering if Mr. Luis just likes to hear himself talk. To my surprise he fell silent, no doubt contemplating the mystifying effects the ball of rock floating in our atmosphere has on such things.

As we approached the last gate leading into the dimly lit Mental Health building, a nurse we'll call Sandy was just coming out. Within a few feet of passing her, she stopped and picked something off the ground. Normally she was a jovial soul so I kidded with her saying, "If that was a quarter it belongs to me." She didn't give me the slightest indication that I was even there, but instead stuck her nose in the air and made a beeline for the gate. This night was indeed turning out to be strange. I then remembered a song from my teen years, "Momma Told Me Not to Come."

Finally we arrive at the entrance of the Mental Health building.

The lock on the door opening is loud like a gun shot in the night. As we step through into the brightly lit room I can hear the screams of the inmates caged in cells down the corridor. We have entered into another dimension, this is the twilight zone. As I walked down the hallway I was able to distinguish some of the voices I heard in the midst of the yelling, banging on metal tables and rattling of cell doors.

Inmate Wille was begging to get out of his cell. His reason for the request was because the air coming through the vent was contaminated with lead and he couldn't breathe. He knew it was contaminated because they, whoever they were is anyone's guess, were burning dead bodies. This was affecting his asthma and he was going to die if they didn't let him out. The nurse was trying to convince him that he didn't have asthma, while the other inmates on the tier were promising him freedom if he would just hang up or bang his head against the wall.

I handed my I.D. card to the officer in the control center and then stood by the huge metal and Plexiglas sliding door. I am instructed that inmate Mike is on the second tier and fast asleep. I breathe a silent prayer of thanks, and wonder how strong the medication was. When I step into the unit several inmates holler out my name like we are old buddies. I remember them more for their acts of self violence than for their names, but wave and holler back like it is a real pleasure to see them. In reality, I am pleased to hear their voices and know that they are still alive, but mixed with sadness that their lives are spent day after day in this hell. Most I wouldn't even recognize if I found myself face to face with them. They are behind sheet metal doors with hundreds of holes drilled into the sheet metal. In front of that is this Plexiglas stained with everything imaginable. I make my way to the second tier where a couple plastic chairs have been set in front of Mike's cell. As promised he is fast asleep. I peel off my jacket, and empty the contents onto the extra chair. For a moment I sit there wondering, catching my mental breath. In my thoughts the picture of the moon comes to mind. Officer Luis has trapped me with his nonsense as I find myself wondering what part the moon plays in this drama. I am filled with compassion.

Francisco Hernandez

Human

Sharp, blue teeth, strong enough to crush flesh and bone; these steel teeth shred everything that is joy and warm. This beast has consumed me, it has swallowed me whole, and maybe it's about to swallow you, too. From inside of this mechanized machine I can see the men and women who pull the levers and turn the wheels. Processing meat like a highly efficient slaughterhouse with no concern for the life it is about to debone. They are hoping to kill my will to dream and keep me from finding a way to rise out from the midst of their schemes. They want to keep me here you see, this is how they make their meal. To rob and steal.

I struggle to find the words to express what it means to be dehumanized. How can you explain dehumanization? How can you put into words the terrible self-worthlessness that is experienced in a system that sees me as less than human, as someone not worthy of human emotion, human contact, or the warmth of a friendship?

I live in a 8' by 10' cage. When people from the outside see where I live, it reminds them of an animal at a zoo. That is how I am seen and treated. I have my shower time, my mealtime, my recreation time, and my work time. My whole life is in their hands; they even tell me how to feel, and how to connect with other human beings. Even so, I am a person who feels and I have my own thoughts like anyone else. I just want to feel like a person and be treated like a human being.

Phillip

Life

Life is a highway
Life is a bowl of cherries
Life experience
Life sucks
Life lessons
Life line
Life time
Life insurance
Life everlasting
Life terms
Life story
Life Cereal
Life or Death
Life and Death
Life Changes
Life cycle
Life flight
Life long
Life style
Life like
Life time guarantee
Life, Liberty, and the pursuit of happiness
For me, Life is a sentence.
Such is Life

Benjamin James Hall

Lockdown

The temperature hasn't broken 90 yet this summer, but it feels rather hot in my cell just now. We are on lockdown; there is no movement inside the prison, save nurses carrying medications cell to cell and the bulls walking the tiers.

When I came to prison, the term "lockdown" took on a whole new definition. I try to think of a good context for lockdown, and all I can hope is some girl somewhere has my heart on lockdown although she doesn't know it. Most of the time we go on lockdown for incidents of violence but today's lockdown is a purpose of an entirely different animal; a pre-violent incident if you will.

The state of Oregon is conducting a practice run on carrying out an execution. Last month the warden told us not to be alarmed, that even though it's been postponed, he assured us his staff will be ready to make sure this execution is carried out humanely with the utmost dignity and efficiency.

So consequently, we are on lockdown! But more than just lock and key, steel making love to steel. We are on lockdown from compassion and humanity to methodically and allegedly humanely, premeditatedly kill someone after spending millions to keep them here for years. My eyes are on lockdown from shedding the tears I so desperately desire to release because pride and ego in the men around me have who they really want to be on lockdown. Their hopes and dreams are on lockdown. My longing for intimate touch is on lockdown; apathy permeates while empathy is on lockdown. It could be that insanity for those on death row is on a fragile lockdown that could explode like shards of metal in a roadside bomb without a moment's notice.

Who people really are in the dark when no one sees is on lockdown. If I had a microphone I would implant it in the warden's head along with the cruelest men I know around me. Then I could hear their unspoken thoughts they have on lockdown then perhaps I could find the key to set them free. We are on lockdown!

Michele Dishong McCormack

National Anthems

September 27, 2012
Essay Competition for the 7th Step Club
Oregon State Penitentiary

My incarcerated friends and students sometimes ask if I voted for Measure 11. While I wasn't living in the state then, at that point in my life, I probably would have supported it. Sure, let's get tough on crime, create a three-strikes-and-you're-out policy, and drive down what I now know is a bumpy and twisted road of reasoning.

That me was a person who had had very little experience with our criminal justice system. However, now that I am inside a Salem-area prison teaching college classes and volunteering at least once per week, I've learned more than I ever wanted to know.

I've learned that a juvenile offender can be sentenced to life in prison for his first crime.

I've learned that a 16-year-old, first-born son has no right to talk to his mom before making decisions about plea bargains.

I've learned that Measure 11 siphons money away from treatment and education.

I've learned that a person can be held in solitary confinement for 6 months without a hearing.

I've learned about and felt in my heart a man's anguish as his mother struggles through cancer treatments, and most roads toward dealing with it are blocked by razor wire.

I've learned that a man might only get to see his sons, the 9-year-old with the green Mohawk and the 6-year-old who has trouble sitting still, just once a year.

I've learned that a man in prison can steep himself in guilt and anxiety and sorrow so long that it changes the shape of his own shadow.

All of this knowledge is powerful. And it makes me think briefly about how easy it would be to not know about the conditions in which my friends, students, and neighbors live.

It would be easier to go back to driving on State Street with the windows down on a beautiful fall day like today, not giving a thought to the 2,000 or so men incarcerated inside an asbestos-laden, 150-year-old fortress.

These thoughts come into my brain. But, I let their cloudy trails pass on by because my life would be less fulfilling and textured if I didn't get to work inside with such articulate, intelligent, and compassionate people.

This connection with amazing people makes it even harder to fathom why our society has chosen to approach criminal justice in such a vengeful and ineffective way, especially when there are so many other models from which to choose. Models that are more effective with recidivism, forgiveness, rehabilitation, and community restoration.

A Norwegian prison in a place called Bastoy is sometimes referred to as the world's most liberal prison. On this island, there are no armed guards, no gun towers, no fences or razor wire. Staff and inmates eat a common meal each day together and take classes together.

When I first read about this prison, it sounded crazy, like something that could not possibly work. But, the recidivism rate is just 16 percent. Compare that to American recidivism rates that sometimes top 60 percent, and "crazy" is suddenly singing a different national anthem.

Bastoy prison governor Arne Nilsen says this: "Both society and the individual simply have to put aside their desire for revenge and stop focusing on prisons as places of punishment and pain. Depriving a person of their freedom for a period of time is sufficient punishment in itself without any need whatsoever for harsh prison conditions."

Nilsen is proud of the fact that no one has been killed or taken his own life at this prison, which opened about 20 years ago. The only gun on the island that houses this prison complex is a bronze statue of a gun.

Nilsen says, "Here you are given personal responsibility and a job and asked to deal with all the challenges that entails. It is an arena in which the mind can heal, allowing prisoners to gain self-confidence, establish respect for themselves, and in so doing, respect for others, too."

I briefly wonder what it would be like to work inside a place like Bastoy with such a philosophy.

Whether just outside of Oslo or with you here in Salem, Oregon, though, teaching and writing inside prison would still be the highlights of my work week.

My students here are, as a group, much more engaged and motivated than students in my regular Chemeketa Community College classes. I always post the highest grades in my prison classes. And I rarely feel a student taking education for granted inside these thick, yellow-drab walls.

When people ask why on earth I want to teach in prison, let alone why I love it so much, it is hard to put into words, even for a writer like me. But, it seems like we cut through layers and layers here. We bore deep into the marrow, straight down to the essence of a person.

A Presbyterian minister, Frederich Buechner, says, "The place where God calls you to is the place where your deep gladness and the world's deep hunger meet." And this certainly does feel like a calling to me.

Perhaps the calling is a bit off-center, dumping me into the rusty, tangled mess of America's system rather than carrying me on strong wings to the land from which my mother's people descended.

Even still, what we are doing on the education floor and in the chapel of this institution makes me feel more like part of the Norwegian system than the American one.

My Norwegian grandmother would be proud and would be glad to meet my students here at OSP.

Benjamin James Hall

9/11/2011

This morning I sat down to read the Sunday paper after a mostly sleepless night in a 100 plus degree cell. Today is the 10-year anniversary of the September 11 attacks on our country. I came across a section in the paper titled simply, 9/11. I skimmed the articles and headlines, looking at the pictures and wondering about their personal stories. There was an older lady who lost a loved one, a Muslim woman who talked about her struggle to live life post 9/11 answering questions about her faith. There was a girl who turned 18 on the 10-year anniversary of 9/11who talked about how each year 9/11 overshadowed her birthday and she felt guilty for celebrating it. Feeling a sense of human connection, I was moved with sorrow and compassion. Later, as I lay on my bunk, the events of September 11, 2001 were on every station it seemed, drawing me away from the football game. I listened as President Bush shared what his thought process was as he received the news, and I felt a great deal of empathy for him, wondering just how tough a position he was in and what it felt like. I watched the footage as the first tower went down, people running and screaming in terror. My eyes filled with tears as I imagined being trapped, calling frantically and screaming for help, but no one would come. I wondered what it was like to live in a country where the threat of terror is an everyday occurrence. I thought what kinds of men do such cruel and evil acts, having no mercy. I've sat in many college classes listening to professors from prestigious universities talk about a sense of humanity of which I felt deeply and identified with as a good thing, but today I wondered about the very word humanity. The bulk of human history is associated with such merciless cruelty and violence and yet people sometimes display such incredible and often unexplainable selfless deeds and kindness but it seems to be the exception to the norm.

Several years ago walking toward the track on the prison yard a guy I know pulled me up grinning as he motioned me with his hand to come look at something. I fell in line behind him on the track and he said, "Look at this kid's back." I noticed a crowd was walking in the proximity and everyone was laughing and pointing. As I looked at this shirtless kid in front of me, I saw a freshly scarred tattoo of a penis and testicles with wings. I laughed along with the crowd but immediately felt a stab at my conscience. I broke off from the crowd but I studied the kid's face, seeing complete and utter fear and humiliation. The story came to me that the kid had snitched on his codefendant. He was no more than 20 and could have passed for 17. His cellmate upon learning of his crime tricked him saying he was going to tattoo something entirely different. Once the youngster had been duped, some older convicts told him he was going to go outside and take off his shirt and walk around at night yard or they would hurt him. I remember feeling such shame for laughing and there was a sick and unsettling feeling in my stomach. I remember thinking we have lost a big piece of our humanity. No wonder many in the public feel we are animals! I tried to imagine how that kid must feel, completely alone and afraid. I wanted to go talk to him and tell him God loved him, but I was too afraid with the whole yard it seemed watching and laughing at him, a test I wish desperately I could retake. What does it mean to be human? Why do we equate it with compassion using the word humanitarian? How is it we are bent on such selfishness and destruction and yet... when I see footage of firemen running to their deaths to save their fellow man or a solider rushing out to pull his wounded friend off the battlefield I feel proud and deeply moved. I believe the worst evil is potentially in all of us but there is also the breath of life, which God gave. There is that voice in our conscience that says, "Don't do this" or "do this." There is that emptiness each of us feels and a voice, which beckons us to a relationship. This is the voice of God. This voice reminds us how much we need Him in order to daily choose humanity—humanity in the sense of how God intended us to live and the way in which we shall live again if we answer that voice, for others.

HJ Walker

Rehabilitation

A minority of the felons that enter the penal system truly desire to rehabilitate themselves. They have repented of their crimes, regret the victims they have made, and wish to makes amends to society. These men find prison blues to be a badge of dishonor. You can always distinguish them from the rest of the prison population. From the moment their feet hit the waxed concrete, they are looking for ways to take accountability. There is a notable hunger in their appearance to get involved in self-help programs. They longed to be a part of the solution and not the problem child.

When their cell doors bang open, they are not headed for the yard, to wander aimlessly around the track, looking for the next prison hustle. They walk with a different swagger. Gone is the tough guy image that breeds violence in gang activities. Their weapons of choice are now pen and paper, instead of fist and force.

They become dreamers of possibilities, believers in goals, faith in second chances. They find confidence once lacked and visions shining bright. School books under their arms and pencils behind their ears. These are the tools that freedom sets before them. Forgiveness!

At night while the rebellious are plotting their next criminal episode, the minority are quietly meditating upon their bunks in their potentials, grateful for that opportunity of another chance, knowing not everyone realizes this gift set before them. A sigh of relief, they lie down in peace, and dream of places not so far away.

Benjamin James Hall

Silent Cries

We were talking about life and death with Sister Helen Prejean; about lethal injection, murder and killers; those seen by many to have lost their humanity. Some of the best friends I call family have committed murder, but their hearts do not line up with the horrible act they once committed, by which society still defines them. The heart is such a mystery. I recently wrote a piece about the heart and the connection between the physical and metaphorical. The heart represents life, a hollow vessel that pumps thousands of gallons of life sustaining blood throughout the body each day. The heart is the center; we often say "the heart of the matter" is this or that. Everything in life has its own heartbeat, a tone and some type of sustaining flow. What does this mean for 2000 criminals inside a walled city?

One cannot miss this big penitentiary that sits off State Street sheathed by four cement walls and guard towers like a medieval castle. This prison, so obviously visible to passersby, yet hidden in so many ways is its own community. Just as every community has its own fragrance, its own heart, so this penal colony has its own heart. The heart of the prison beats but it doesn't always pump life. I walk around entombed inside the confines of this living and dead heart. Although my travels are limited, my feet have and continue to beat the pavement of these dimensions again and again, taking the pulse of the prison. There are so many voices, mostly loud, boisterous and aggressive but faintly, indeed often indistinctly, I hear the silent cries. Near the softball diamond there is cheering; there's an assortment of activity in this section and some vitality. Cutting off the track, my feet touch down on the asphalt of the handball court. Somehow this area of the heart seems harder and darker. I pass by the many soldiers standing shoulder to shoulder, their faces colder. Iron masks of pride presumably corresponding with their hearts…and yet…I always sense deep within the recesses of the hardest heart that fear and ever so slightly, there it is again, those silent cries. Moving back to the track I turn aside my eyes from their watch. Would that I could be invisible so that I could study each face. Maybe I could see what lies behind the masks of cold stares, somehow reaching past it and touching the lost dreams, deferred hopes and tears falling behind their eyes. Lines are drawn in the chow hall, and benches, tables and weights on the yard! Everything about the geography of this camp seems to separate us, locking us out of one another's lives hiding behind lies.

There are other places in the heart that don't beat so cold. I ascend the stairs through the pathways of the heart, passing the descending infected blood cells of souls devoid of hope to the education floor. In class with my friends, you feel as if you're walking across the hope and aspirations under construction compartment of the heart but always some fear. The silent cries are louder in this section and louder still as I walk into the chapel. So much so that the silence has transcended and is capable of being heard in some cases as it's being healed. This sanctuary feels the softest and safest place inside the heart's chamber allowing you even to see outside and beyond your confinement. There is peace and joy in this part of the heart, but the deep silent cry always lingers.

The visiting room seems a different heart all together. I sense happiness, hope, longing to fall into the remaining space between you and the one you love, and fulfillment mixed with sorrow. In the visiting room there is a silent lamentation of another kind, that of a mother's heart broken, wondering where she went wrong and a child's pain of not understanding.

The heart of the prison beats on as night seizes hold, taking this place captive. Those dreadful cries are now the loudest. Two thousand diverse pulses, silent anguish and torment as quiet tears of regret and shame and hopelessness tarnish pillows. The heart of this prison is broken, but God's grace is pouring through the cracks like a healing balm for those who would look for it. Grace brings peace to the silent cries.

SP

The Conclusion

Drama arises ever so often, because our hearts are so invested
Now we become offended easily.
We fight hard
But the deep love we have for each other
Is unseen to the untrained eye
For some reason I feel like things have changed
It could be because I now live thirty miles away
behind a thirty foot concrete wall
The convenience that helped us stay in one another's orbit has vanished.
My words, my feelings, and quick witted jokes
spewed out from me without a second guess
Are now contrived.
Everything is critically thought about, therefore, inauthentic
I want so badly for things to be like they were before
But even I know that is a joke.
For that moment has long since passed
There is no hope in reviving it, not even briefly.
Your life has changed as has my mind.
Where do we meet?
My habit of accommodation coming to an end
I'm digging in deep to keep this stance.
Reproach is what I feel, more so than you'll ever know
And I will never tell
I am very proud of me
because now I know when some things are bad for me
How to let you go.

Francisco Hernandez

Beyond the Wall

Nestor Diaz-Miller

The Creature

The subject of mass incarceration needs far more time in further deliberation. Although the sentences have been and still continue to be tried and carried out, they have already been pressed into action. The misappropriation of credible information has had a lasting comprehensive impression. The potter's clay has made a mold of madness and mayhem.

How do we combat the cold creature of incarceration? This sadly seems to be the place where familiar faces fade away in fear of recognition. Personalities desperately disappear into desolation.

I am a refugee of my own regrets and remorse. Old concrete walls, rusted iron bars, and razor sharp barbed wires have become the home for the hopeless. Struggling to cover the lies, searching to find safe haven in this immense mayhem most don't mind calling home. The constant overwhelming anticipation of the next inevitable feeling of dehumanization. My only looming impatience is for the hope of this so-called justice not to work against us.

Are we the people no longer salvageable? Are we not ready and capable to maintain stable lives and confront the labels that trap and entangle us? For us, for them, for you, we shall continue to pay our dues.

My mind has been filled past the brim with the reminiscent memories of my life before this LIFE. They have all but become daydreams of what if's, maybe's and endless possibilities. The countless forks in the road of life. Choose life, choose death, and I chose. Sometimes knowingly doing what was wrong regardless of the potential repercussions. Choosing substitutes rather than antidotes.

In this environment where success is measured by rates of recidivism and the reinforcement of rehabilitation. The only true source of positive transformation is within oneself. Through self-assessment, self-awareness, and genuine selflessness. The only estranged form of treatment we endure is one of a categorizing nature.

Prejudice and stereotypes are the giants we attempt to strike down with the weapons of knowledge and wisdom. The actions of most seem to dictate the behavioral skepticism of all those in a position of power.

The cynicism of society seeps and lingers throughout time and only continues to be exasperated by the media who in turn mislead people to then depict a picture of ignorance.

What can we do to change the views of the world? My focus is to clearly speak to those who are willing to actively stand from their seats and fully engage in the resurgence of a movement lost but not forgotten. The cause being to lend aid to those that lack the capability and the resources to overcome this cold creature of incarceration.

I call it the creature due to its ever growing size and its beast like tendencies. It's ugly when you are trapped inside the belly of the beast, in the wastelands of the wasted and wicked.

I fear not for myself, for there is hope on the horizon for me. My fears reside for the hopeless and the voiceless. For those that have accepted the losing mentality.

Who is willing to help them? Who will get their hands dirty? I am among the fire and flames. I am willing to help the scorned. Raising awareness to the problem is the first step of many. Now it's time to move forward. The Question is, are you with me?

Benjamin James Hall

The Phone Rings

The phone wakes me from a short few hours of sleep and her voice is the most soothing alarm clock to my ears. I don't want to go to bed early or sleep in late for fear I will miss a moment of life's exuberant ecstasies. Who wants to sleep in when the day is meant to be conquered in adventure, seeking out the exotic colors of creation climbing the mountains of taste and stepping into the waters of learning for the first time, trusting loving touch without fear or apprehension?

Yesterday we were all together for the first time in 22 years sharing the same plates of food after the streams of salty joy flowed like Niagara Falls. We all laughed as my dad's OCD kicked in picking up the trash that could wait till later for us. Others went to sleep, but I remained awake long after the summer sun had dropped into the nothingness of the western horizon, my first sunset in a new setting in so long! I finally drifted off to sleep in the awkward comfort of a new bed and I dreamed of her.

To hear her voice on the other end of the receiver seems still a dream as she says, "I'm taking you to the beach." The drive is mostly silent, her left hand on the wheel as her soft right hand gently squeezes my awkward clammy hand. The landscape is a loveliness nearly forgotten, traveled to only in my mind most years of my adult life. Upon arriving, it's as if we're at the edge of the world, the sand and lapping waves between my toes are like waves of peaceful elation. Every now and then I look around thinking the police are going to come arrest me for excessive happiness, or perhaps my sense of restored autonomy, but each time she leans into me, her touch and fragrance reassuring me this freedom is real. That night, lying on a blanket in the sand, lit with a fiery red sky, water shimmering, I just don't have or need words.

The obnoxious clang of her cell phone ring breaks the natural sound of the wind and waves, and my eyes open to the angry, mechanical bell and the pursuing yell of, "WORK LINE!" Reality hammers in; I'm late for my prison job. I will tiredly climb the 66 steps of which the 17th steel diamond cut rung is loose when stepped on with enough weight. I wonder how much it will matter when my feet no longer touch down on these steps in 8 years. Will my dad be alive, and will her name, her smile, her eyes, and her touch still be just a mystery to me?

Benjamin James Hall

Wasteland

Walking across this dark landscape, there are not many places to go but so many faces, all different yet somehow the same. Sometimes I make eye contact searching for kindness or a friendly smile but all I see is fear masquerading behind pride and callous coldness. Once they called us the "condemned" which we wore with shame. Now they live it as a badge of honor, as a choice glorying in their shame here in this wasteland, a scene of destruction, confusion, and a wilderness of hopes and dreams, lost time and blown talents unlimited. Bodies covered with ink like Samurai Warriors of old only minus the courage, bearing images of torment and death. Flaming death heads, double barrel shotguns pointing down forearms above dripping syringes full of liquid death that covers fear and pain. Guard towers with bars and barbed wire; tear drops under the eyes, gravestones, skulls and cross-bones. Words that read whiskey bent, hell bound and momma tried. Here in this burnt-out desert many will fight at the drop of a hat showing great false courage but they surrendered long ago. They bear nicknames such as Guilty, Crazy, Brain Dead, Criminal, Damage, Toker (RIP), and Murder Man, banners of hopelessness. They are the walking dead here in the wasteland. I feel tempted to hate them! But sometimes, sometimes… I see behind those cold eyes just a flicker of longing, sometimes, I am looking into my own eyes and I realize, this is someone's son, someone's father. Once maybe a mother cried for them the way mine cried for me.

Love

Brandon Davila

#19

A young man imitating the greats, stepping to the plate, bottom of the ninth in a tie game, bases loaded, full count with two outs. No pressure, after all he is playing on a diamond. The pitcher winds up.

Who gets the game winning hit? The one nicknamed The Kid or Big Mac, The Iron Man or The Big Hurt? How about an all-time great, who plays for the team and city on his uniform, not the name on the back of his jersey. The hometown hero, destined for the Hall of Fame.

A walk-off grand slam would be great, but a run across the plate will win the game just the same, reach base on a hard-hit gapper, talkin' to the press post-game lookin' dapper.

The young boy with dreams of big league teams linin' up to capture his talent, watches patiently as the tennis ball rolls down the roof, knowin' it will bounce oddly when it ricochets off the gutter just like a Ryan Express cutter. The fence is callin', grand slam is enticin', but he waits, waits, waits and drives it, slices it off the garage for a walk-off win, a World Series title in hand!

#19. No nickname needed. An all-time great, truly one of the best to ever play the game. San Diego is a bright and amazing place, made brighter by his smile, a smile that was always in place! I am honored to have imitated and mimicked such a man, such a professional, a true role-model.

Not too many players in today's game can do the same and I feel bad for today's kids. Not too many to choose from when you're pickin' who to swing as, going for that walk-off win….. Rest in Peace to an All-Time Great, #19 Mr. Tony Gwynn.

R.I.P to all the greats who taught me to hit, throw, catch, shoot, and win like a professional. Thank You!!!

Nestor Diaz-Miller

Brick by Brick

As this heart beats with a steady calculated rhythm of a song, I can only wonder if it is a song even worth hearing. It is a song that many have tried to hear, but only a select few have actually listened to. With every moment that passes, this heart longs to be heard.

As this song tries with all its might to find a way out, it is met with walls of protection. Walls that have been raised up over time to help lessen the blow of being hurt time and time again. But now they are a hindrance, only serving the purpose of getting in the way and muting this ever-beautiful song of the heart. These walls, of all the false tall tales of this so-called love, have got to be taken down brick by brick.

For how am I to allow people to get close enough to even hear this song if my past whirls of emotion will not let anyone get a front row seat? This heart of mine is damaged, battered, and bruised, yet still young and full of life. It is a strong and caring heart ready to love and be loved once again, to cherish and be cherished forever.

This heart is addicted to love like a sick heroin addict with no money. Yes, I need my fix. Or like an alcoholic with the morning hand trembles. Yes, I need my drink. It is important to know the difference between needs and wants. The truth behind that statement rings oh so close to home because I know that I don't just want love, I need love. I need love to feel alive, for without it I might as well not feel anything at all.

This heart aches to break the confines in which it has trapped itself. I refuse to allow this heart to remain in ruins. I will not let myself continue to sweep my emotions under the rug. I have to share my heart.

My family and my friends deserve me to be as open and honest as I can be. I can't just smile through the rest of my life anymore and expect to build relationships on lies. I must be assertive in taking on the challenge of being genuine, and I shall. So that this song may be heard.

Brick by brick, these walls will be taken down. Slowly but surely, my heart is free once again. No longer allowing the past to dictate the future, but rather just being in the present and enjoying all the things this life has to offer.

Francisco Hernandez

Fusion

Indescribable is my heart for you.
When I wake up you are with me,
When I lay down you are with me
My heart is one with yours.

Uncomprehending love like the spin and twist of the Milky Way
The unknown center where does it go
Crushing gravity, forces pull, and twist my heart.
Pain.

Unknowable beauty and glory stretching across the universe
Blazing and traveling at the speed of light.
Nuclear reaction; atoms consistently splitting into eternity
Fusing my heart with yours

Brandon Davila

I Want

I don't just want to tell you that I love you
Every day I want to show and prove my love
I don't just want to kiss you goodnight
I want to kiss you awake every morning
I don't want it to be me and you
I want it to be US
I don't want to dream about our tomorrow
I want to make your dreams come true
I don't just want children with you
I want to watch our grandchildren blossom
I don't just want to dedicate a song to you
I want to be the one to write it
I don't just want to hold you
I want to never let go
I don't just want to make you giggle
I want to do something about it
I don't just want to be your today
I want to be your tomorrow
I don't just want to be your forever
I want to be your eternity

kosal so

meditate

i am a revolver hard-pressed against the temple
spilling sinister thoughts all over the shrine.
it's like dirty thoughts in a clean mind
and the heap of feral fantasies create tension
that needs liberation.
it's like a criminal breaking into my head
and my head becomes the penitentiary.
when will my mind demolish
the construction of prisons?

who i am without you is the burial plot
for the body of an unwanted bomber.
i know,
i should learn to pray for modesty
and meditate
to calm the layers of palpitations.
there is a calm i do not know
through anyone else.
but how do i find you
in this forest of maze?

through the canopy of trees
i've argued against the ocean.
i've tried talking to walls

and to myself.
i know,
i'm never going to be normal.
when will my mind divest
the condom of solitary confinement?

my deepest me
listens for things other people don't hear.
but more than the cacophonous conversation
i crave the pleasure of feeling myself.
i need you, to keep me sensitive.

Nestor Diaz-Miller

My Wine

Sitting in the sand ever so sensual, staring off into the setting sun.
Repeatedly reciting my proclamations of feelings to my one true love.

My lips graze upon your cheek,
with the provocative purpose of giving you pleasure.
The gentle tantalizing nibbles on your neck,
release the soft moans of emotion to further.

Stimulate the stirring senses.
Curious fingertips wander around the body to be noticed.
Passionate, romantic endeavor everlasting soon to be adjusted into
    focus.

Welcoming warmth of bodies and souls collide time after time.
Destined to climax, grasping for intimate desire to feel more than
    alive.

As the time runs its course each day, our bond only heightens in
    quality.
Much like the finest of wine, only time will become our relationship
    remedy.

Aiming at your heart with whispers,
Promises of our long time becoming our forever.

Nestor Diaz-Miller

Unconventional Fairy Tale

The very first thing that catches my eye is her unforgettable smile. The type of smile that puts all others to shame. Next is how she looks when she is truly happy. The type of happiness that makes the world a better place. All those times when she really does laugh out loud. Through all the stresses of the world, somehow I can always get her to crack that ever-beautiful smile.

As I continue to stare at her, I notice my vision working its way up towards her eyes. So full of joy and adoration. My oh my, how many a man has fallen to a lesser beauty than that of which these windows of the soul contain. The color cannot be described as just a color. It is difficult to even say they are only eyes, for that constrains their mysticism. Those eyes are so vivid and full of life. They are inspirational and encourage me to continue living with my eyes wide open, so that I don't ever miss the beauty in life.

I have lost myself in those eyes before. Every moment I don't spend losing myself again I feel robbed of my potential happiness.

I know one thing for a fact: she is my fairy tale princess. She is the one trapped in the tall tower all alone waiting for true love's kiss. Waiting in a land far away for me to come and rescue her from the dangers of the land of the unknown. The beast that keeps me from her is prison. I am a captive of my own demise, but I will conquer this creature of confinement one day and will be with my princess. I will take the hand of my beloved and make her mine. King and Queen to be hand in hand when the time is right.

From the luscious hair to the perfect smile, I will indulge and lose myself in the eyes of my princess. I strive to be her ever-victorious knight in shining armor. To give her the kiss of life, to awaken her mind and soul, her body shall follow in due time. This evil curse of pain and agony is one of a self-inflicted nature. My own failure was my fall from grace, but now I have risen from the ashes of my previous shortcomings to become the man I was born to be.

This is my fairy tale. Never to be written by the people of the land, but rather by the prince that has failed time and time again to reach the castle of his dreams. I shall write this with the tip of my sword, and I will continue to let my heart bleed on the pages of my life. Here is to the hope of a better tomorrow and my happily ever after. My day will come.

Nestor Diaz-Miller

The Room

As I begin the journey into the room, I must get prepared. For I am about to enjoy the next several hours of the day with the one and only love of my life. My shirt, my pants, and my shoes have to be clean, pressed, and pristine. My hair has a tendency to match too. The long trek down the tier and down the stairs to the office is filled with anticipation for what is to come. The elevated heartbeat begs to be noticed. That anxious feeling of happiness has yet to dissipate, not even a little bit.

Then comes the processing into the room. They ask me the usual questions followed by the usual answers: name, number, any property and I respond with my name, my number and a clever remark about a ring: "nope, not yet, but hopefully soon." I check in as fast as possible so I have time to spare. I like arriving before she does so I can enjoy all the little things that happen when we meet. After checking in comes the long walk down the short hallway to the door that leads to another universe. The escape hatch to a world within a world. It is where I can get away from the everyday struggle. Much like the C.S. Lewis book, this is our getaway, our secret hideaway, our wardrobe so to speak. Time seems to freeze and we both become ageless. This place has turned into our sanctuary and our meeting place. This is where we met for the very first time and where our best memories have come into existence.

I enter the room and find one of our favorite seats. Each seat has a different memory attached to it. Then I wait for her. I see her walk through the door, and she scans the room to see if I'm in the first section but she knows I'm normally in the second section.

She lifts her head, and at last, our eyes meet. My life seems to make a lot more sense in that very moment, and it will not soon be forgotten. She lights up, she smiles, and then she walks even faster towards me.

My mind races with thoughts of what if. My heartbeat begs to be noticed. We embrace as if it might be our first and last moments together. We seem to somehow find refuge in one another's arms. We catch ourselves staring at each other, smiling and declaring proclamations of who missed whom the most. Then with a subtle movement, I lean my head in towards her to give her a gentle yet provocative kiss.

We then find our seats and hold each other's hands, fingers interlocked. Staring just to stare, laughing for joy, and I show her all the gratitude for everything that she does for me.

In that moment, I am free. In that moment, I am alive. My only hope is that we can keep those precious moments continuing for the rest of our lives.

kosal so

the war of beauty

not many things on this earth to adorn
or enhance my face more.
you found a way to pry open a smile
oppressed by decades of war.

my concept of compassion is adolescent,
but you have taught me to kiss
all the creatures on your limbs.
now my heart's a mirror
reflecting your passionate temper.

why would i focus
on the strategy of war
with all the beauty i have seen and touched?
but if you don't find enough fabric
to veil all your beautiful limbs,
i cannot promise i won't attack
all the innocent latent creatures.

my concept of compassion is adolescent,
but my hands are at service
and my lips
want to befriend your skin.

Nestor Diaz-Miller

This Sky of Ours

You are my ever shining, everlasting, ever radiant sun, and I am much like your moon, for I am nothing but a cold, dead, and desolate object. A deserted rock without meaning. With an unchanging lifeless exterior with little to no purpose. You bring me life. Life to my meaningless existence.

You brighten my days and illuminate my evenings. Every moment I'm not with you I can't help but count the seconds until I get to see you once more. My entire existence revolves only around you. You are my day and I am your night.

Together the world is our playground. The only time the moon is ever blocked from the sun is when the world gets in the way. That is why I always make you my priority as we dance among the clouds, precious to those gazing upon our tragically beautiful romance. For we can only see one another from a distance.

We represent the beginning and the end of days and nights. We both come from separate ends of the spectrum. We meet in the middle to engage in our romantic ventures. You allow me to reach for the stars. You remind me of your beauty from every sunrise to each sunset.

You are honestly more than my other half. I am only but a reflection of you. When you fall, I am there to lift up the remains. You are my illumination, my motivation, and my inspiration. You mesmerize me with your deliberate persistence and your greatness.

Together we shall remain for the end of time. Our journey has been in the making since the beginning of time. Our union is a once-in-a-lifetime event. Our love shall eclipse everything. Night and day, I am yours forever.

Mom and Family

Charles C. Hammond II

Chimes in the Wind

Gusts of wind blow, causing the clang of the wind chimes to ring out in the distance, drawing my focus: a subliminal message. Birds chirp, oblivious of time and circumstance only seeking to live another day, to sing their song that they were meant to sing. Playing a role in my mind, escaping to what once was so many years before.

The fragrance of the vast expanse of floral delight fills the air, alluding to a pre-summer's day. Sun-kissed iced tea in a pickle jar on the back porch, sunbathing sisters to torment if I choose, and the anticipation of the cool, wet, and refreshing swimming hole right at the edge of town just on the horizon.

There it is again: the wind chimes beckoning me home from exile. My mom on the back porch, cigarette in one hand, coffee in the other patting the concrete steps bidding me come to enjoy the warmth of the morning sun rays and the warmth of her heart seeking my company.

Delight crosses my face momentarily as I hear her voice as she calls us in from a long day of play for dinner, and then the dinner triangle when we take too long to respond. Ding-ding-ding-ding-ding. The closer we come, the louder it gets. The anticipation of one of her experiments causing our mouths to water, knowing that most of them turn out to be pretty good.

As I run towards the ringing of that old triangle, somehow it begins to sound more like a school bell ringing. Now I realize that I'm hearing the chow bell ring, and the scent that I smell is no longer

Mom's cooking but whatever resembles food in he chow hall. Still, I find myself searching for the call of the wind chimes in the breeze and my mom on the back porch, hand held out for me to come home.

Charles C. Hammond II

A Mother's Love

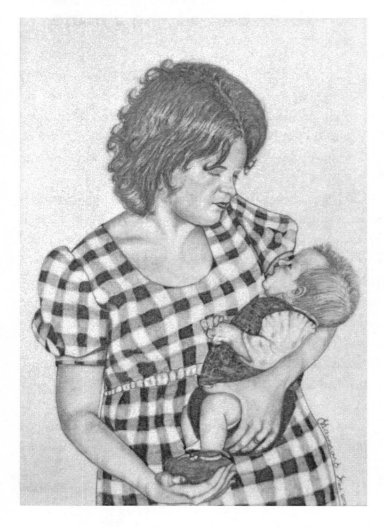

Charles C. Hammond II

The Answer
on the Other End of the Phone

My finger begins to dial a number. Not sure of who may answer or what type of response that I will receive, I wait for the system prompts to complete the call. There is an answer. The almost monotone feminine voice explains what to do: "If you want to accept this call dial 5 now. If you want to know the cost of this call dial 8 now. If you do not want to accept this call, hang up." To my delight, she chooses to dial 5.

"Hello." An elderly lady's voice beckons. It's my grandmother's roommate who has been a family friend since I was about 12 years old. We exchange pleasantries all the while remembering when I used to go over to her house to do odd jobs for her son (who later became my uncle) who drove big rig trucks for a living hauling hog fuel, lumber, and the like. I would clean out his trailer, wash the truck, and whatever he could think of beyond that, for a fee, of course. Nevertheless, it was the breakfast that Helen would cook for us all with a pot of coffee to wash it all down with, along with the great conversation, that I cherished the most.

"Talk to you later, here's your grandson," Helen says after our farewells and talk to you later. Immediately after my grandmother gets on the line I hear a familiar "Hello." Frail but determined, her voice speaks out waiting for my response.

For the first ten minutes of the thirty-minute call, she asks how

I am and if there is anything new. Although she repeats the inquiry multiple times, I oblige her. Sometimes with the same answer, and sometimes not; either way it seems to be new and fresh for her.

For the next twenty minutes, she explains how she still shakes from nerves, and she is ready to go home to be with Jesus. She tells me, "Don't you cry for me, boy." I tell her that I won't promise such a thing, but there is nothing left unsaid between us so I am content with what we have left.

Next thing you know that same monotone voice says, "You have one minute remaining." How rude! Either way, we say our goodbyes and I am forced to wonder if this will be our final goodbye. So I say, "I'll see you either here, there, or in the air, but until then I love you and will call the same time next week."

With that our phone call ends, but my week is complete in knowing that I had one more day with this wonder of a woman. Although next week I will still be unsure what type of response I will get or who will answer, I will call again.

Charles C. Hammond II

Better

45 years. Almost half a century living, breathing, laughing, crying, and aging was all brought to an abrupt stop after a yearlong battle. Often, with tears in his eyes, my father softly speaks of my mother, how he loved her, how he misses her, wondering how to live life without her there by his side. Trying to hear and relinquish his mournful disposition as many try to comfort him by saying it will get better; he can't look beyond her pain to something far better. Today, tomorrow, yesterday has no flow, no color to brighten the sunrise signifying the new start that he craves.

He says, "It's bullshit son!" to me as he begins to rewind the day's reflection upon how many times people have said that his pain will pass. "I will forever see her face in the moon as it passes overhead. The stars twinkle as she passes by carrying her sweet voice to my ears, telling me of her love that surpasses the expanse of what is seen every night. I will never forget! I don't want to."

What can one say to remedy the unhealable, the loss of one's identity for the past 45 years? Only the indistinguishable groan of the spirit as it cries out in pain for the loss of what can never be replaced can capture but a degree of what can never be spoken or understood.

To be better is relative to what can be gained by a loss. So really, what is it? I lost a mother, but he lost a piece of his soul that only remained within the heart of his cherished love.

Nowadays, there is no reason to rush home to an empty house that now remains silenced by the voices that used to fill it. What's next? What's better? "No son, I will not, nor could not ever forget."

Charles C. Hammond II

My Most Cherished Moment Is...

Stepping out of the transport vehicle after an hour-and-15-minute car ride, that still seemed to be at warp speed after 20 years of not being in an automobile, I was overwhelmed by emotions. After 20 years, I was finally home, my sick mother's arms outstretched towards me to the left, my father directly ahead of me, tears in his eyes, with a phone to record every moment. As my arms strained against the hard, cold steel of the cuffs restraining me and the shackles on my ankles assuring the two armed guards that if I ran they could easily catch me, my mother's hug set me free.

Although I was lost in the moment and the gravity of the circumstances in which I was standing there, what was in my mind the most was the fact that I had to pee and could hardly hold it in any longer. I had realized, moments after we left the prison, that I really had to go, but it wasn't like I could ask them to just pull over at a gas station or something. Reluctantly, I asked if I could use the facilities and with a chuckle the officer walked before me to check to make sure that there were no files, cuff keys, or someone waiting in the wings to spring me. He checked till his heart's content and said at long last that I could proceed. Ahhhhh…, sweet relief. To explain how tricky it is to use the facilities while you're cuffed and shackled is difficult, but at that point, I was at my home, using my bathroom, with my folks just a few feet away in the living room, so I really didn't care.

The interesting thing that I noticed right off the bat is that everything was a whole lot smaller than I remembered. The rooms were smaller, the kitchen table was shorter, the toilet was a lot closer to the floor, but somehow, it was still the home I remembered.

As I walked into the living room where everyone was waiting for me, Dad on the couch just across the room, Mom on the couch to the left, the officer just ahead of me, tears began to flow down my face as I realized that this was going to be the last time that I would ever see my mother again. Bittersweet as it was, I was blessed to have the opportunity to be there. I sat down right next to my mom, and even with the cuffs and shackles, I hadn't felt that type of freedom for so long that I had forgotten what it felt like to just kick back on the couch.

There were multiple moments of heartfelt goodbyes and reassurances of my wellbeing until my real homecoming finally arrived. It only seemed like moments later that the officer said that we had about 10 minutes left. At that point, the officer reached over to release one of my hands to be able to hug my mother. I immediately reached for her and was met by her touch that I had yearned for since the day that I was arrested. I buried my head into her embrace, and up until that moment, I had kept most of my tears in check. I lost it. I wept that deep guttural sob that you can't control even if you wanted to. We stood up to embrace one last time and she began to pray for me. Then after she asked God to protect her baby for her, she turned to the officers and thanked them for their kindness, then began to brag about how proud she was of her son. Once again, I completely lost it and sobbed without a thought of who was watching, or what they may have thought of it. I bent down to kiss her one last time, embraced her frail frame, and whispered to her that I loved her and would see her again someday. Then, just like that, it was over and I once again found myself in the back of the transport car heading back to my confinement.

It was all so surreal. I could hardly hold on to it all, yet it was one of the most memorable experiences of my life that I shall never forget. Sadly, it was the last time I was to see my mother alive, but someday I shall see her again, and once again I will bury my head in her embrace and remember that at that moment I am truly free.

HJ Walker

A Father's Love

I have been in and out of juvenile facilities, institutions and prisons since I was fifteen. My father's footprints have always been etched in the sand next to mine. It was unconditional love for an ungrateful son. I am sad that it has taken me so long to realize his heart for me.

My first stint was a juvenile facility called Vermouth Boy's Ranch. Every opportunity for visits he was there, bringing my mother and siblings. We never talked much; as a matter of fact we never talked at all. But he would work all week, come up for visits on weekends and bring a bag full of goodies.

At eighteen I went to the San Bernardino County Jail in California for one year. By this time my family had moved to Oregon, so visits were out of the question. But I never lacked for canteen money. When it came time for my release I had a plane ticket for Oregon, a house to go to, clothes to wear, and a vehicle to drive.

Within months I was in trouble and on the run from the law. I would run to my old stomping grounds of California, or to Texas where I had distant cousins, or Arizona to an older sister's place. In each case when people tired of my bullcrap, bus money for Greyhound tickets were sent to come home. Until I was finally apprehended and sentenced to five years in the Oregon State Correctional Institution.

Like clockwork my dad made sure I had regular visits and money for canteen. Still we never talked as he sat with my mother and siblings across from me. After five years he was the one to pick me up. Again opening his home for me, buying me clothes, and providing transportation. He now began to tell me, "Boy we are at the end of the rope here, don't mess up this time." Within months I was on the run. Again California and Arizona, again bus tickets were sent, even though I had left him financially strapped. This time was different, though, as my crime was a capital offense. This time I couldn't go home.

When I started my life sentence, there he sat across from me in the visiting room of the Oregon State Penitentiary. Still bringing my mother and what siblings were left. But now I had fathered a child myself that he was providing for, but things had changed. This time I at least was man enough to say no more money for canteen, I would find a way to survive.

My mother passed away while the rest of my siblings found lives of their own. Eventually, even my child married, moving on herself. But across from me in the visiting room my dad continued to sit. One day in my shame and guilt for putting him through so much undeserved crap I said to him, "Pops it is not fair for me to continue to ask such sacrifices out of you. You need to move on and finally live your life free of me." He looked at me and simply said, "Boy, you are my life." Today those words still choke me up.

In all these years of visiting, I didn't know this man who continued giving me so much of his life. He was a stranger, and I had been so ungrateful. Who was he? What were his likes and dislikes? Did he believe in a God, did he have any faith at all? Everyone else had pretty much faded into time, but he made it clear that he wasn't going anywhere. So I hatched a plan. I decided that it was time we talked.

Excitement filled me when I learned of his next planned visit. When he arrived we had our usual greetings and small talk. Like a couple actors, we gave each other a manly hug. We shook right hands, pulling our shoulders into each to touch. Not too close, not too tight, and definitely no touching cheeks.

We sat down, had the polite formalities of asking how each other were doing. I was filled in on the latest family news of who was doing what, that they all send their love, miss me and were planning on coming sometime soon. I blame myself, but still after years of hearing it, that crap got old.

Next on the agenda was the normal routine of the vending machines: purchasing cupcakes, potato chips and soda pops. Stuff to fill our idle mouths with. Usually from here we would get into the conversation of politics; another tool we developed to distract until time ran out. But while we were opening our soda bottles and chocolate cupcakes I said, "Pops, I got something I would like to talk about." He looked a little apprehensive; probably from the last time I told him that he needed to move on.

Before he could respond I plunged right in. I said, "You have been coming up for years, sitting across from me, purchasing goodies. But do you realize that we really don't have a clue about each other. Oh, it is obvious that you love me, but who are you? If we are to continue visiting don't you think we should get to know each other?" When I finished it felt like the room grew strangely quiet, and sweat rolled off my forehead. Finally he said, "Okay boy what do you want to know?" My dad and I begin to talk.

Since that day the journey has been one of the most wonderful experiences of my life. My father and best friend is one amazing fellow. That visit was well over a decade ago. At 80 he is no longer able to visit, but it's not because of a lack of desire. My only regret is that it took me so long to say those simple words, "Hey, who are you?"

Benjamin James Hall

A Mother's Heart

The greatest gift I ever received on this earth was my mother. It was her tenderness that came from love. From the time I was a boy to now, her compassion was evident. The time I cried when George shot his handicapped friend in *Of Mice and Men* and I did not understand, my mom patiently explaining to me it was just a movie. How she always seemed to give way more than she ever had, I will never know! Softly reading me stories of *Curious George* and the *Cat in the Hat*, singing to calm my fears. By some means my mother always sees the best in people, even the vile. Some would say her kindness is naïve, but I know it to be a supernatural gift. Even to this day her compassion flows through the phone to this prison when I am distressed. When I got older and joined a gang participating in horrible acts, I remember this inside force given to me by my mother, which kept me from crossing certain lines of cruelty. Each time I was cruel, inside I was tormented. Compassion and tenderness: I learned these traits from my mother; there is no one like her. No one could ever be what she has been to me, and she truly has a mother's heart, a gift from God. Although I only received but a portion of it, over the years it served as a compass of compassion for others. I guess I am just a momma's boy. I think it's why words can crush me so much; they are her language of love, just as they are mine. It's one of the reasons I'll never understand cruelty and just plain meanness, although I've participated in both. My mother's gift of tenderness has helped me to have compassion for many, even the cruel. It has enabled me to stand and listen to someone no one else would listen to. In those times I fail because of fear, or indifference, God reminds me of the gift He gave me in my mother and brings my heart back around, along with a little advice on the phone to look for the best in others. My mother, I know that she would move heaven and earth to help me if she could. Once on the phone, my mom asked if my friends do anything for me on my birthday in prison. I replied, "Yeah, they punch you real hard in the body." My mom, love her heart, said, "Well that doesn't sound very nice." My mother, I love her. She loved me when I was unlovely, vile, and undeserving, giving me her time, tenderness and compassion. One thing is certain; I have never felt like a motherless child, and I will keep striving to make the gift she gave me a bigger reality.

Nestor Diaz-Miller

Best Friend

How do I even begin to write about you? Surely, this pen to these poor pages will not properly do your story justice. No matter what I share on these few lines, people will never know what you mean to me. Letters to words, words from feelings, feelings from actions. I just want them all to know about the one and only mother I consider my best friend. I will pour out my heart and express my thoughts. I will say what I mean and mean what I say.

The bottom line is that I love you. You showed me the true meaning of love with the way that you raised me. Actions over everything else. From the very beginning our bond has been unique in comparison to all other mothers and sons. We starved, we struggled, and we stayed strong thanks to you.

You were a teenager, and I was a toddler. We were so much the same in regards to how scared we both were at what we were facing in this big, bad world ahead of us. We had to learn our own way through the labyrinth of life. We had no idea what the world held for us.

Through our entire journey, one thing has always been true, we were not alone. We always had one another. That was all that mattered. From those early days you taught me the value of family and loyalty. To forget all the irrelevant, materialistic possessions that this cold world has to offer. All those distractions that have a tendency to blur the vision and distort the needs of many. Not to allow anything to hold any dominion over us.

When the money would run out and there were no meals to be

had and nothing but hope in our hearts, we still had each other. You always kept us going with your persistence to not give up. You would always say, "We can make it through, so long as we have each other."

Now it is been over twenty years but still your words resonate with me today, just as they did then. We may have grown up, but my heart is still filled with the hope you instilled in that young boy so long ago.

I know now that love is about sacrifice. You sacrificed all to give me the best life that you could. I will never forget what you did for me. You have always been my pillar of strength and I, your anchor. We kept each other in balance, as we still continue to do today.

I will still strive to make you proud. Your baby son has grown up now. Now that I am a parent, I will encourage my children the same way you did for me. I will show them the love they deserve, and I will sacrifice my blood, tears and sweat to ensure their happiness and wellbeing forever.

The words that remain in my mind until the end of time will be: Love, Loyalty, Sacrifice, Strength, Perseverance, and Patience. You are, and have always been, my dearest and best friend.

HJ Walker

A Letter to Mom

Dear Mom:

Laying here in this prison cell I am full of regrets. I wish I could talk to you like I've never done before. You were barely a half of a century old when you passed away. I never saw it in my selfishness, but today I know my life took its toll upon your heart. In our last visit the pain in your wrinkled eyes is etched in my mind.

Where are you? Are you in heaven? Can you see me? When I talk to you can you hear me? Do you know these regrets of your child's heart? When I was young you would affectionately rub the top on my head with your labored, cracked hands. Momma, I need to feel your touch today. I miss you so very much.

I am so very sorry! Wherever you're at, do you get to understand this? Do you still spend hours on your knees in prayer for me? Out of nine children I consistently broke your heart, but you never got tired of laying it down. I was a great cause of it being broken. Does my life today help mend it, is it possible to heal a broken heart, I sure hope and pray so.

Momma, I need you to pray for me one more time. I need you to pray that I can know your forgiveness. Momma, I hurt so very much. Would you pray for me one more time and ask God if we can talk. Mom if I can just hear your voice of encouragement, telling me not to take life so serious.

Wherever you're at, I am still your boy and I love and miss you so very much. I will make you proud of me. Rest in peace!

HJ Walker

Hero

Alcohol and drugs have blurred my childhood memories, but I am sure like all kids I had super heroes. I watched cartoons, longed for a Batmobile and Superman cape to be under the Christmas tree. I was mesmerized by the Road Runner, but must admit I rooted for the Coyote to catch him. Casper the Friendly Ghost was cool, but I didn't prance around in his costume on Halloween.

Through the teenage years *My Favorite Martian* and *Lost in Space* were watched religiously. But I never aspired to be an astronaut. *Planet of the Apes* was a box office sensation I snuck in the Fox Walkin Theater several times to see, but the only acting I've ever done was acting remorsefully when busted doing wrong. The spaghetti westerns like *The Good, The Bad and The Ugly* were the bomb. Clint Eastwood made millions I would imagine. My mother attempted to dress me up like a cowboy, but I sure wasn't having any of that.

Music played a tremendous role in shaping my perceptions. I lived the rock-n-roll lifestyle through bands like ZZ Top and Alice Cooper. I was a *Fool for the City* (Foghat), always getting the lead out (Led Zeppelin) and felt that I was born with a six gun in my hand (Bad Company). In that era of time there was a song for every occasion. LSD trips while cursing the Misty Mountains, beer drinking and hell raising, and taking the slow ride in love making. But the closest I came to becoming a rock star was in my head on my air guitar.

My older brother was someone I greatly envied; he was the picture of success in a criminal sort of way. He was no Al Capone, but he and his buddies were a set of good fellows. I idolized him so much I would stand in the mirror practicing his cocky grin. Wear my shoes down so I could walk bowlegged like him. That didn't make my parents all too happy, but after contemplating this life sentence I wouldn't vote him into any hall of fame.

It was my brother I attempted to imitate, but it is my dad I see in the mirror. He wasn't able to spend much time with me, having to support a wife, eight rugrats, and at times half the relatives. I understand now why he drank so much and appeared to be so angry all the time. Even with so many parental dysfunctions in his toolbox, which today would have locked him up, I know he cared. He worked two, sometimes three jobs just to put Spam in a can on the table.

Although my dad has pulled plenty of Felix the Cat magic tricks out of his bag, he is no cartoon character. Never a movie star, but he played the greatest theatrical drama in raising nine antisocial kids. Wasn't an astronaut, but kept the plumbing working even if the shower was a garden hose at times. Definitely never a rock legend, but to this day some of the things he instilled in me are music to my ears.

If anyone in my book deserves to be my hero it would be him, because with all the crap he had to put up with raising nine ungrateful kids, he still epitomizes unconditional love. Not one kid has he abandoned no matter how ungrateful, in my heart he is a true hero by any account of the word.

kosal so

homage to her feet

she could have killed the seed that sprouted inside her belly.
the nine months it took before it was born
she could have wished for a miscarriage,
she wouldn't have to go hungry to nourish its roots.

in return the son gave her pain and contraction,
saliva, vomit and urine.
but she wrapped her precious treasure in delicate sarong,
carried him through war-wounded soil,
her feet worn and torn from dirt, rocks, hills and mountains,
from twigs, thorns, foliage and forest.

she could have left him for dead
on the side of the road when rebels gave chase.
instead she left behind her culture and tradition:

i was the child that she embraced.

seventy-five hundred miles across the ocean,
her feet peeled and bled from sand, salt, reefs and rivers,
from shrubs, marsh, broken glass and asphalt.

a story is told of a prostitute
bowing at the feet of the messiah,

weeping and wiping them with the hair of her head,
kissing his feet and anointing them with perfume.

billows of wasted tears flood the room.
i am my mother's flesh and blood
locked behind concrete and bars,
without the chance to wash the feet that carried me.
the feet that are now aging with scales dry as the desert,
the feet that have endured time and the elements.
so I cry these words for all sons and daughters to ponder:
pay homage to your mother!
her feet are tired.

HJ Walker

Knock on Heaven's Door

Man may have come first,
From Adam's rib you gave birth.
Because of sin, fruit is produced from the toil of man's brow
After a season of nine months you gave birth somehow.
Your toil of labor pains does not end there,
For a life time of worry you did bare.
You cuddled, held dear and constantly prayed,
You saw your dreams of your child slipping away.
You agonized for the labor pains that began in your heart,
Wondering what happened to your child with such a bright start.
I wish you were here to see your life of labor was not in vain,
I wish I had a chance to acknowledge your pain.
To thank you for a life time of sacrifice for me,
To know your boy has become the man you hoped him to be.
I believe you are in heaven and able to witness these things,
So I know,
You now know my present pain.
The pain of not being the child, the son, the man,
Or friend you longed for,
The pain of having to wait
For heaven to open this door
Mom I love you…

Francisco Hernandez

Letters

I have always had an incredibly close relationship with my mother. I remember as a child how affectionate and loving my mother, Andrea, was with me, and my brothers. Even so, I think she used to confide in me the most, and she always let me know how special I was to her.

Recently we were having a conversation about how much my sons have grown up. Throughout the years since I have been incarcerated, my mom has helped raise Matthew and Frankie, and has been an excellent grandma to them. However, in this conversation she told me that to her, my sons were like her own children.

She treated these children, who were my responsibility, like her own children because of her great love for me. I can say that without a doubt, no other person, man or woman, up to this point in my life, has ever sacrificed more for me than my mom. She has followed me to hell and back. And we have gone through the valley of the shadow of death together from my father's craziness, to my life messes, near death experiences, and complete hopelessness. To our lives now walking with Jesus Christ together, we are now more than just mother and son, but also brother and sister. It's ironic because she held me up when I needed it, and now, I am strength for her, and hold her up when she needs it.

One day my mother will be gone, but I will always carry with me her hopeful and loving words. Her words and love that sustain me and let me walk through the valleys and hills.

I've received letters throughout the years while I've been incarcerated, and most of them I don't have anymore, with one exception; my mother's letters, I've never thrown one away. I keep them because they are my mother's beautiful words written with her beautiful hand, her enormous spirit, her amazing heart that wrote those life-giving hopeful words to me.

When my mother is gone, no hope will be lost, for I know that we will see each other again. Moreover, she will live in my heart and in my memories as a child kissing her from her head to her toes, and I will have her paper, ink, words, letters.

Francisco Hernandez

Looking Over the Wall

I have 6570 days of looking at the gray drab Oregon State Penitentiary wall. At intervals towers stand, mirrored windows enclosing the lone sentinel inside. This place has a medieval fortress look to it. I am now wondering if it has the medieval feel to it. What did those people feel long ago when there was little light in their lives, and their only concern was to survive the famines, the bandits, and the plagues?

I don't have to worry about famine. However, the bandits here are the gangs, and the prison politics that all are subject to, which act like a net waiting to capture the next weary fish. "Fish" is what they call the new arrivals into the prison. The first questions the fish hear are, "What are you in for, let's see your paper work, what gang do you run with?" The right answers let you pass through to the top, and the wrong answers push you to the bottom and make you subject to the bandits.

The plague and sickness that most have to worry about here will not make your flesh rot (or mostly not). This plague attacks the spirit; it is called the plague of hopelessness. It tries to infect everyone; it tries to creep in like a larva burrowing into an apple. Some let it in without a fight, and some simply swat it away only for it to come back again. Hopelessness is relentless and many have fallen victim to it. You can see the scars of it, tattoos on the men's faces, things that say "your society is not for me." The scars of needle marks that inject the placebo of kill-your-life meth. It gives the false hope of escape, but only lets the sickness sink deeper in.

The vaccine for hopelessness is different for some, the same for everyone. An example of a pill that has helped me is when I would climb the ladder in the laundry that led to the catwalk far above all the workers and the madness of below. It was my ritual early in the morning to look to the west. There it was, so beautiful it left me breathless. The brilliant sunrise. Beyond the gray wall. Colors that I could never recreate in my paintings. The beauty of it mesmerizes me, yellows that transition to oranges, to reds, and violets. More shades and hues in that instant than could ever exist.

As I am looking over the wall, all my mind can think about is God; how could anyone not? I feel the upwelling of hope. Such beauty that God has created, such beauty that gives hope. I think about how everyday God's mercies are anew. I think about how one day my loved ones and I will see that sunrise without the wall. Until then, I continue to look over the wall every chance I get, even if it is the sky.

God blesses me so that I can have hope. God is the vaccine for hopelessness. My family gives me hope as I think of summer days by the Clackamas or Sandy rivers. Rivers that we spent countless times by in years past, enjoying food and each other.

God has blessed me with an amazing family and in many ways. This is why I can say no to the gangs, no to the drugs, and no to hopelessness.

Benjamin James Hall

Meeting Jackie

I met my second cousin Jackie yesterday for the first time since she was a little girl. The last time I saw her was in a picture and she was just a small child. We have been writing for a while. Jackie feels comfortable sharing her life with me since she knows I will not judge her, she says. They pull me from a writing workshop in the chapel and the visit is unexpected. I am a little disappointed to leave the workshop but excited when I find out it's Jackie. As I enter the visiting room I see a slender auburn haired girl sitting with her back to me. I approach, knowing it's Jackie, and I'm reminded of the array of emotions I've felt for years for Jackie and her sisters without even meeting them.

I think about Collin serving his 20-year sentence for the years of torment he put Jackie and her sisters through. When Jackie was big enough, she fought back, so Collin had his friend hold her down. What was wrong with this guy who couldn't even admit what he did and had no remorse? I am one who believes in forgiveness, but it's hard! Every day you get to get out of bed when really maybe someone should have just put a bullet through your head. But I don't want to think about Collin right now. Jackie looks up and gives me a nervous smile as we shake hands. It is always a little uncomfortable in person for the first time, especially inside a prison. Jackie is tall, beautiful and only 21 years old. We talk like old friends cut from the same fabric of life, exchanging family war stories and laughing about our aunt's mannerisms. We take two photos together, one for each of us to keep. I am so happy to meet her but my heart begins to feel heavy as she speaks of the "brothers" referring to an outlaw motorcycle club she runs around with. Lifting her shirt, she shows me a tattoo I've seen on countless other convicts; it is a pistol on her waistband the way gangsters do. My heart is broken as I leave the visit because I see what she cannot, the end result of a lifestyle that takes your beauty and sucks dry your vitality leaving you betrayed and alone. But I'm not going to be pushy. I simply tell her, "Don't let anyone abuse you, cousin," that she is family and always has a place with me. We hug and she tells me she will come again. On my way back to my block, I push my anger for Collin down. One thing I know for sure, come what may for Jackie, I'll pray for her and I will be there if I can.

Brandon Davila

Momma Knows Best

Where do you think I get my quick wit, my affinity for sick kicks, and the fact that I don't watch my lips? You know, speak my mind, be blunt, tell it like it is, drop the F bomb whenever the need arises, and trust me: that need exists. I made it today because she paved the way. Showed me how to be a man and taught me the game. Not the game per se, but the game all the same. Taught me how to treat a woman with dignity and respect, open doors and pick up the check. She'd yell at the refs when they stacked the deck, nobody is gonna' cheat her baby boy. Spoiled me with toys, oh the joy over my Lion-O action figure, oh boy was I spooked when I threw it into the air, dropped and watched it shatter. So I hid it, in the dirty laundry hamper. She got madder over bad grades so I did better. My first tattoo two simple letters, B and D, our same initials, mother and son. She is my best friend, the only one. Love is such an easy word when it comes to my feelings and emotions. I love my mom; she is the sand to my ocean. I am proud to be her son, always have and always will, that will never change. So when you get sick of my mouth she is to blame.

My Forgotten Aunt

The sky was filled with dark gray clouds, the wind was swift. The rain was constant and this is what I consider to be perfect weather. I find that I am the most productive on dreary days like this one. I suppose that is why I finally walked to the Hostess discount store, something I had been meaning to do for a long time. It was only a little ways off from my after school program and I was craving a six-pack of crumble donut holes. Once I was in there, I saw a pack of orange slices that triggered a memory of my aunt.

I had an Aunt Olivia, but to us was known as Faye-Faye. She was one of my favorite aunts, always giving me sweet treats, taking me out for tasty eats, and she was always giving me compliments that I could never get enough of, like, "Tah-Tah you sure look handsome today." She was someone who had credibility when it came to knowing what looked good. Back in her day she was too hot to trot, with that famed Farah Fawcett hair-do, and white lipstick. She was a trendy lady, but later struggled with the disease diabetes. This shifted her priorities. The orange slices reminded me that she lived right across the street from the Hostess store. I felt horrible because although I knew her health was rapidly failing, I never followed through on the vow that I had made to myself in regard to my aunt.

During the previous Christmas of that year my parents, grandma, siblings, Dominick and Maxwell all had exchanged gifts, and no one was disappointed with what they had received. As family began to arrive, it became apparent that we had had a more enjoyable Christmas than some of our other relatives. I see my auntie Faye-Faye and she is overjoyed to see me, as I am to see her. She is visibly struggling to breathe, her legs are extremely swollen, but her familiar, beautiful smile masked all of her ailments. It only took a little while for her to ask me, "Did you get me anything for Christmas?" It only took a fraction of a second, for the lie "Of course" to fall from my mouth.

I quickly ran upstairs to my mom's room and told what had just happened and how bad I felt. The truth was, I never saw my aunt often enough to know that she would even make it to Christmas dinner. I offered up the idea that my mom should let me give the Estee Lauder perfume that I had bought for her to my aunt. Without hesitation my mom agreed. To see the way my aunt reacted was priceless. I imagine that she truly thought that I had remembered her on Christmas. I vowed to myself that I would start going to visit my aunt more often, especially because she didn't live that far from me.

I rushed out of the Hostess store and headed towards my aunt's house when a boy Terrance from high school stopped me. We weren't exactly friends but not total strangers either. I told him I was headed somewhere and to my surprise he asked could he go.

Once we arrived at my aunt's house I wasn't sure what to expect. She was not really mobile so I expected the apartment to be in sort of a mess, and it was. Dishes piled in the sink, food spoiled in pots on the stove and clutter gathered on the floor. "SP, whose house is this," Terrance asked. I didn't answer instead I picked up a picture frame that seemed to be the only spotless thing in the entire apartment. Inside the frame were my cousins Elishua, Akin, Yelafa, Neila, and Rolando, all standing in front of my aunt's past homestead. My aunt was pleased that I had stopped by and glad that I had brought along a friend. She told Terrance that she was pregnant with nine children.

This was believable because her belly had become extremely swollen and hardened. She commanded that both of us come over and rub it. While she and Terrance talked, I went to town cleaning her studio apartment. Once I finished, Terrance and I left and my aunt seemed to be as thrilled as she was on that Christmas day. It was as if she was so happy that little Tah-Tah did not forget about her. The truth is that I had often forgotten about my aunt. I was too preoccupied with the trivial clique dramas of high school. This is something I always feel terrible about because the next time I saw my aunt was at her funeral service.

Michele Dishong McCormack

Other Mothers' Sons

Curious George story before I tuck him in.
Warm milk for restless nights.
Hand-made quilt with frogs around a blue flannel edge.

Two cells could fit in his modest room
with its hand-me-down dresser.
Two narrow metal beds.
Two thin scratchy blankets.
Two metal chests of worldly possessions.

Are those mothers' sons
hungry,
cold,
happy,
sad?

The 501st visit from James's mom
on his 4,381 day
falls on Thanksgiving this year.

Thanks, Mom.

James M. Anderson

The Gift of Discovery

I was introduced to the gift of discovery at an early age, and it's left me with a treasured memory of my grandfather who has long since passed. This is a short story about him, and how my favorite memory of him came to be.

My grandfather's name was Otto. Otto Joseph Anderson. He was a quiet, intelligent man who rarely talked. A fisherman who loved to hit the local waterholes after a hard day's work at the Gerber knife facility, usually returning home with his trusty green 10 gallon bucket nearly full of small mouthed bass and bluegill. Well, that's how I remember it anyways. Though I found them immensely annoying, my grandfather loved his dogs Mitsy and Spot. They had a pungent smell, they barked nonstop, and they were clearly two mutts that only an owner could learn to tolerate, trust me. My grandfather was a methodical thinker. Someone who knew how to get out of a bind. When uninspired by my grandmother's cooking he'd discretely call Spot and Mitsy under the table and feed it to them when she wasn't looking. Ha-ha, so much for those mayonnaise salads. Another example of his methodical thinking was having me blow into the alcohol monitoring system that was attached to his car's ignition when he wanted to take me fishing.

My grandpa Otto was well known for three things. The first thing he was known for was being an accomplished race car driver back in his younger years, which was clear to anyone who saw the incredible amount of trophies and photographs adorning the walls of his home.

The second thing, and unfortunately the saddest, was that my grandfather was an alcoholic. When I was seven years old, for example, my grandparents took my older sister April and I to the state fair in Salem, Oregon, to watch a Johnny Cash concert in the fairgrounds amphitheater. The year was 1986, and although I was young, I distinctly remember the people around us screaming excitedly for Johnny, "the man in black." It was clear that he was a hero. Later that night, while still at the fair and contemplating within my mind how Johnny Cash had become such a hero, my grandfather punched my sister April in the face during one of his drunken episodes. He was hauled off to jail immediately and my sister was taken the opposite direction towards the hospital. I don't know about hero, much less deserving of a distinguished title such as "the man in black," but it's important to note that this isn't a story about my grandfather's issues with alcohol as much as it's a recollection of my favorite memory with him, so let me get back to the third and final thing that my grandfather was most well known for: being an excellent carver. A jack of all trades if you will.

I can clearly remember that in one of the back rooms of his modest three bedroom home in Gervais, Oregon, he'd often disappear for significant amounts of time to work on his projects. Projects that we all knew about, but that were rarely spoken of until their completion. Oftentimes I would listen patiently in the hallway, first door to the right, wondering what exactly he was in there building and wishing that I could somehow be a part of whatever it was. I would hear sand paper swooshing back and forth rhythmically like strong winds to an eroding hillside, tools being picked up and sat back down with clangs and thuds, and the occasional word to himself, such as "ha, got ya" as he undoubtedly worked a piece of difficult material into its required position.

This brings me to my favorite memory of my grandfather. It was a hot and cloudless early evening back in the summer of 1991 when he took me out to St. Louis ponds to test the sailboat he'd spent months carving out of a single piece of wood.

That summer evening at St. Louis ponds was amazing. A day that will live forever within my mind as a wonderful memory of who my grandfather truly was when immersed in his comfort zone. Not a drunk memory, not a bucket overflowing with fish memory or even a race car barreling down the speedway at breakneck speed memory. No, nothing as simple as that. This was a memory that a shy and reserved young child such as myself holds onto forever, mostly in the hopes of recreating a similar memory for one of my own children or grandchildren down the line.

You see, what I mostly remember about my grandpa Otto is the sailboat story, a simple day that made a lasting impression on my mind and one that I'll never forget. I just hope that I'm able to retell it with the same vivid detail that I saw and felt that hot summer evening while with him. I was at Grandma and Grandpa's house after dinner that late afternoon and, out of the blue, Grandpa asked me if I wanted to take the sailboat he'd been working on out to the pond to see if it would float. After I quickly nodded my head yes, he brought it out of the back room covered in a blue cloth. We walked outside and proceeded to load it carefully into the trunk of his car, all the while telling me that I was in for a big surprise. On the way out to the pond he explained that the sailboat was for me and that I would be taking it home with me later that night… if it didn't sink that is. I couldn't believe my luck. I couldn't believe that all those noises behind his locked door were made working on a project meant for me; I was thankful and beyond excited.

At the pond minutes later, I remember kneeling down beside the water and allowing my fingertips to break the surface, anxiously feeling the excitement within me swell knowing that at any moment the sailboat that I had spent months inquiring about would finally find its home within the same gently flowing water that danced around my fingertips. As Grandpa leaned down and carefully removed the blue cloth covering from the boat, revealing its beautiful blue paint and immaculately stitched white sails, he looked at me coyly with his unlit brown cigarette dangling limply from his lips and said, "You ready to see how she sails boy?"

Of course I was ready! I was beside myself with anticipation and swimming in the realization that these were the moments that all grandchildren dream of when they're growing up: solitary trips to foreign places where the magical world of exploration and discovery were revealed. A place where skills were gained through the wisdom of a grandparent and experiences were ingrained and preserved in memories concrete.

I paused for a few seconds and studied my grandfather's gray stubble chin, wondering curiously about how many crazy roads the old man had traveled. I mean, there had to be some pretty interesting stories in the creases and wrinkles that mapped his forehead. I mean, you don't get a breathalyzer installed in your car unless you've gone through some stuff, ya' know? I asked my grandpa, "if the boat doesn't have a motor, and if it's not connected to a string or something, then how are we going to get it back, how will it know to come back to us?" Grandpa just laughed while lighting his brown cigarette and mumbled something about trusting in the wind to bring it home. And with those words, those simple but assuring words, he knelt down with the sailboat securely in his weathered hands and gave it a shove.

I was terrified that for some unknown reason the boat would just up and sink, maybe get grabbed from below by one of the mythic water creatures that all twelve year old boys conjure up in their minds as if they're absolutely real. But our sailboat was different. It was strong and built with expert hands that didn't put up with failure and therefore well beyond the grasp of some washed up pond creature. Well, if they were real anyways.

After the boat left his hands it took on a life of its own. It immediately took off toward the middle of the pond, slicing through the water effortlessly as if captained by an experienced seaman. The wind, as if on cue, began to pick up and the sails whipped back and forth beautifully, its white strips of cloth silhouetted perfectly in the rippling waters background. Pond ripples were hit head on and the miniature crests were defeated by the hull's knifelike sharpness. The sailboat looked magnificent, a piece of art floating effortlessly through the water as both its owner and designer stood on the edge of the pond grinning with exhilaration.

Grandpa Otto patted me on the shoulder as we watched our boat and quickly said, "We better get over to the other side of this pond before we lose sight of it kid, let's go!" He skipped off anxiously and I was left to follow. It was easy to see that he was proud of his project, and I felt honored to be with him on its maiden voyage.

Over the course of an hour or so, Grandpa and I made several trips back and forth around the pond to reposition the sailboat and again send it on its way, but what we also noticed was that the evening sun was slowly slipping below the horizon and that it would soon be gone. Just when we decided to call it a night and pack up and head for home, the wind abruptly stopped, leaving our boat stranded dead center in the eerily silent waters of the pond. We stood there for several minutes as the light continued to diminish, hoping mightily that a sudden gust of wind would provide enough push to get the boat to shore one last time, but we soon realized it was a hope for another day.

After about a half an hour we were standing in complete darkness, moon casting jittery shadows across the surface of the water, sailboat still drifting in the middle of the pond as if lost at sea. Grandpa was shining his flashlight across the water, his eyes squinting noticeably as he searched, mumbling something inappropriate for my young ears. After a long couple of minutes the silence was finally broken when he turned to me and said, "You don't want the boat back tonight, do ya' kid?" He couldn't be serious! I was mortified thinking that such a beautiful boat would be left behind for anyone to grab first thing in the morning and quickly responded, "Of course I want it to come home with us tonight, Grandpa, what should we do?" He smiled reluctantly and explained that due to the circumstances there was only one thing we could do.

He told me to hold out a hand as he began to remove his clothing. Piece by piece he tossed his clothing across my outstretched hand until he was completely naked, which surprised me to no end. I have to be honest with you and tell you that I was clueless as to what his plans were. I even wondered if that was the moment I had always heard of, you know... when an old person goes crazy and loses their mind requiring permanent housing in an old folk's home and life-long dates with diapers. Thankfully I was wrong. He put his flashlight in my free hand and sternly told me to keep it pointed towards the boat roughly thirty yards offshore. Holding my grandfather's clothing tightly against my body, I struggled to locate the boat with the flashlight shaking nervously in my hand.

Without warning, I heard a huge splash and felt drops of pond water hitting my face as I realized that without hesitation, while I was fiddling with the weak beam of light, Grandpa had dove head first into the water. When he surfaced, gray hair slicked back with pond moss and who knows what else, he looked back at me and yelled, "On the boat, I'm blind out here, get the light on the boat so I know where I'm going!" I worked the flashlight back and forth across the moonlit water until I located the lonely looking boat. I held it there steadily as my grandfather worked his way through the murky water towards it.

All around me I remember hearing a symphony of frogs croaking loudly, birds chirping in the distance as they sang their nightly good-byes, and crickets seemingly all around me announcing their presence with their fluttering wings. "Ha, got ya'," my grandfather yelled out from across the water as he clutched the sailboat on the underside of its hull. He started pushing it slowly in the direction of the shore as he swam. Excitement coursed through my veins wildly as I realized that the boat would undoubtedly be coming home with us after all. As he neared the edge of the pond, obviously winded and panting hard, I noticed that the animals seemed to instinctively know that a catastrophe had been avoided and at once they erupted into a chorus of wildlife cheers. I dropped the flashlight to the ground and lowered myself to the water's edge, inch by inch the sailboat was getting closer to the shore. Relief poured over me as I scooped the boat into my newly freed hand and hugged it tightly against my chest. I have no doubt that Grandpa saw the appreciation evident in my eyes, but he paid it no attention as he shivered over to his pile of dry clothes.

Grandpa quickly dressed and we walked around the edge of the pond laughing to ourselves about the night's ordeal. At the car we dried the sailboat off slowly in the illuminescent light of my grandpa's trunk and covered it again in its protective blue cloth. We were careful not to damage its overworked sails or snag it with the shredded edge of the cloth.

When we arrived back at his house my grandmother was waiting expectantly at the door, curious as to why we'd be at the pond well after sunset. Grandpa Otto dismissed her quickly with a short, "Ahh, you know, a little fishin', a little boat sailin', easy to lose track of time." And with that he disappeared behind the hallway door, surely with the intention of starting another project fresh and new.

Grandpa wasn't the most outgoing man in the world; he surely wasn't "the man in black" by any means, but that summer night he became a hero to me. I'll never forget that experience or question its worth in terms of how I've managed to view his legacy in hindsight. He made mistakes, sure, but he also left a lasting impression on all those that he came into contact with, and isn't that what we all strive for? Isn't that the goal we all set out to achieve? Through my grandfather Otto Joseph Anderson, I was able to discover redemption and purpose in a life mixed with promise and bad decisions. I discovered that no matter where I'm at, whether in prison, or with my own future grandchildren at the water's edge of St. Louis ponds, I can make a difference that lasts a lifetime. Thank you, Grandpa. Thank you for the gift of discovery. I miss you.

Brandon Davila

Time Bomb

Since day one
You've had my back like a spine
And when this time came
You tried to take the blame
We both knew was mine
The biggest crime
Was that I was never the son you deserved
You moved Heaven and earth
Gave me all you were worth
Prison and cancer, gift and a curse
Each a bit of both
In their own odd way
We both count days
You want more and I'd do anything for less
Stress fills my chest where my heart used to beat
Blessed for I am a man now
No longer the boy I used to be
F the C, cuck this fancer
Still every visit is filled with laughter
Still we shed a few tears
They gave me years
Said you only had months
What was it? Somethin' like 6
Who's lookin' sick now?

The haters that's who
Hatin' on you because of your sick tattoos
They're sick because of my ill kicks in my prison blues
Breakin' news this just in
I'm on my way out
My life's ready to begin
No end in sight for your life
The one they claimed to be in sight
We both fight
We both bleed, kick and punch
Eat bad news for lunch
Snack on B.S. like a bunch a Crunch n' Munch
Keep an appetite for growth and change
Stay thirstin' for knowledge
A SID number to you
To her a son in college
A man she is proud of
To me the world's greatest mom
Our 15 minutes is about to blow…BOOM
TIME BOMB!!!

Other Thoughts

Charles C. Hammond II

Blah Blah's

A small coffee shop/diner just off Burnside, dull and lackluster during the day, waits in anticipation of the evening's cadence. Round about midnight till just before dawn it becomes the after hours lounge for the underground nightlife of the city of Portland, Oregon.

The freshly fried stench of burgers, fries and the like mix and mingle in the air with clouds of smoke and the low rumble of banter between customers as you first cross the threshold of this throwback to the 50's type diner. The first thing you notice is the highly shined black and white checkered floor that leads to a bar with a row of red upholstered stools that line the length of it, a couple of 50¢ pool tables, and booths that wrap around the outer perimeter of the rest of the joint.

To see this during the day, dim and full of yuppies sipping their coffee just before work would throw off anyone who comes just after the clubs shut down for the night. Whoever sang "The Freaks Come Out At Night" must have come to Blah Blah's just before they wrote it. Colored Mohawks, painted faces, chained outfits with piercings in places that would make a grown man weep. Liberty spikes, Gothic apparel, and eyes showing an utter defiance of authority.

What a place of obscurity, showing diversity in a place that once brought order to chaos. This is my place of refuge, my place to fit in. Allowing my Mohawk to fly and be commonplace as I eat my burger and fries to wind down from a night of debauchery. This is my freedom, my choice, and my sanctuary. This is Blah Blah's.

Charles C. Hammond II

Under the Surface

Years of reflection, confronting emotions damaged and skewed by abuse and neglect seemingly yields understanding, reconciliation, and wisdom. Just under the surface, a response lingers hidden away from the light. Twisting and turning, burning and yearning, awaiting release yet biding its time for the perfect moment to unleash the tension for all the world to witness.

Ugly as it is, the emotion behind the curtain lives on and continues to pull levers blowing smoke to cover its tracks, tantalizing the fringes just outside the peripheral, often causing one's demise. Nope, it's still there!

They say the dog that you feed the most wins; well, what of the dog that others feed? You put up a sign to stay off the grass and to not feed the animals and next thing you know there is someone having a picnic right in the middle of the lawn throwing raw steak to the bears just on the other side of the fence.

What a world we spin within ourselves, allowing a playground to be built where the wild runs free and the tame become lost in translation. Bound or free, you choose. A leash is only as effective as the one that wields it.

SP

A World I Call My Own

Walking through by and by, passing through many different worlds, yet not caring nor worrying about the next man's troubles. I'm just all focused on me and what's going on in my own little cosmic world. A boy crying because his father has just smacked his hand for misbehaving, but soon his hoots and hollers are silenced by the treat that comes from Daddy's pocket. All the while I don't miss a beat. I continue to strike. Unfazed by all of the commotion in the streets I strike. I strike past the silver statue man and I strike past the homeless man with a sign that reads, "Can you please help, homeless and want to buy a fifth." He hollers out, "Hey can you...." And before he finishes my feet have carried my body past him without acknowledgement, not concerned about the worries or troubles of the next man. I am totally consumed in a world that is all mine.

Approaching my destination I encounter a light-skinned man with the afro. I wish that I could avoid him but he is standing right on the corner of 5th and Broadway, the exact location of the entrance to my destination. So I brace myself and continue to strike, just a little more swiftly than before, and without failure the light-skinned man with the afro says, "Hey Brotha" and I don't say a word. I just continue to my destination and just as I'm swinging the glass door open he yells, "Brotha, is that how it is?" My thoughts force a smirk on my face. My reply in my head was, "not only is this the way it is, but how it will always be because I don't know you, man." I was not concerned with him or the humanitarian cause he was trying to get me to sponsor for twenty-one dollars a month. It almost upset me but then I remembered that the only things that matter are the things that pertain to my world and I, and all those thoughts of him were quickly gone from my mind as the sweet smell of recycled department store air blew in my face. Suddenly, I'm standing in a place that is all too familiar to me. On my left are the women's shoes, and to the right women's perfume, and immediately in front of me are women's handbags that fascinate my mind, less because of their design and style and more so because of their outrageous prices. But hey more power to the chicks, cougars, and women who can afford them, after all it ain't trickin' if you got it. I head to the other side of the department store. I'm not picking up anything for myself today, only scouting for the greatest gift ever for my mom for Christmas, which is 25 days away. I finally settle on what seems to be the most perfect gift that I know will blow her away. I was extremely amped and filled with joy until I spotted the spirit killer who is the light-skinned man with the afro.

I walked out of the double glass doors and head to the cross walk and right before I step in the street he says, "Hey that's a nice coat…" and before I could indulge in him buttering me up, he slapped me with, "these kids could survive in weather like this, if they had a coat like that!" I stopped and smiled with delight because I can appreciate a good backhanded compliment. All I remembered was, "that's a nice coat." And after all, it was a nice coat. It was my favorite charcoal colored, double stitched, three quarters length peacoat that I had received the previous Christmas. When I opened it and put it on, I kept it on all day. While holding hands about to say grace my cousin said, "You know you can take that coat off now," and my mom asked me, "Are you really going to eat in your coat?" With these happy memories floating through my mind something in me changed, after all it was the season to be jolly and give back.

I walked towards the man with the afro and allowed him to give me his spiel about how I could help feed and shelter a child, even though I had no intention of committing to 21 dollars a month or any dollars a month because that sounds like signing up for a new monthly bill, and, at 21 years old, all I can do is give a one time donation, and that's what I did. After leaving him I ran into a different homeless man holding the same, "Can you please help, homeless and want to buy some whiskey" sign. I smiled and gave him a few dollars. Just as I'm reaching the parking garage I see the original sign holder and as I reach into my pocket to get some loose bills I say to him, "Hey I seen your friend up the block!" He smiled and said, "Yeah there's a group of us, we're just trying to survive!" He thanked me and I finally got to my car. As I sat there I realized that I felt super good and not so much from purchasing the best Christmas gift ever but more so for the interaction that I had experienced. I thought it was neat that the men were honest about wanting to buy liquor in order to stave off winter's harsh nibbles. I'd too rather be cold, drunk, hungry and numb versus cold, hungry, and feeling every bit of winter's wrath. I realized that there are other things outside of the world I like to confine myself in that are just as important and that it is more than okay to step outside of yourself and immerse yourself into the worlds of others from time to time.

Jon Killoran

Alone

```
----------------
----------------
```

Status: online	**Hello?**	
Error-check code accepted		Is anybody out there?
Running diagnostics...	**I'm so lonely...**	
0486211739405276		
421134205138115		Where are all the People?
1016141265681615		There are images of what they
2372827152640751		did, what they liked, but not
Calculating...		where they went
Primary Solar Panel: 86%	**Hello?**	
Secondary Panels: offline		People like water and trees
Backup Power: standby		but I don't see any. People like
Detect Collision – Imminent		cities, but I see only ruins.
Calculating...		Where are all the People?
Plotting New Course...	**Hello?**	
3...2...1...		Where did they all go?
Engage 2 second slow burn		
1410562315753909	**I'm so lonely...**	
6779812004165843		There are images of what
Thrusters Disengaging		People wondered – art, God, love
Adjusting right ascension		
35° 17'		War – and what they held in awe
Uploading communication relay		-Hydrogen into helium and the
Relay status: 17%		Geoglyphs, Empires and the
5956337914156882		Grand Canyon.
1933624731020199		
Relay status: 43%	**Hello?**	

Error-check code malfunction
Shutting down...
Communications relay: Offline
7696371013105121
1165271414761260
0124756897665422

1312621871344919
2447653865312214
3201078937421247
Diagnostics complete

System: Operational
Calculating...

I see coordinates, but
People see names, saw time.
seconds, minutes, millions of
years; what is time? A name?
Hello?
Do they know where People
went?
Do they know where they are?
Hello?
Where are all the People?
**I'm so
lonely...**

Is anybody out there?

SP

An Induced Mind

Sitting in my work area with a dreadful feeling gripping my motivation, I soon resume the role as a seven-dollar-a-day prison worker. Sluggishly, I put on my hand-me-down heavy leathers, thick gloves, ventilation mask, welding hood, and my coveted work jeans that I have grown sentimentally attached to. It's six-twenty-three in the morning and winter's jabs are penetrating my bones. I begin to create a burn barrel's warmth in order to comfort me.

Bored, my body settles into an auto pilot mode with my welder. I need some stimulation so my mind starts to wonder. It becomes less like work and more of me seeing what kinds of designs I can make out of the weave patterns. My filler wire at the top of my welding gun becomes like the majestic wonder of before time as it slowly inches toward my grounded metal. I wait patiently then it happens, The Big Bang. The spark of the arc creates puddles of bright orange matter that will only coagulate once it has cooled down and becomes solid metal. The embers of orange fireballs act as stars that have escaped the grips of gravity. Their heat titillates my lap as the stars crash and burn. Fast moving fireballs fry my flesh but fleeing isn't feasible, nature and I morph. I circle around and around, expanding the puddles as Dark energy expands the universe, lost in awe. I know embers have rained down upon my leg but the sensation of these fast moving molecules have extended their stay. I flip my hood up, throw my welding gun all in a panic, then I reach for the Jokisch and extinguish the fire. "Damn, my favorite jeans are ruined," I say to myself. The displeasure quickly turns into delight. The jeans already had gone through the "natural" process of distress with snares, wears, tears, and washes but the fire added a special touch. They had taken on a vintage look identical to jeans that easily cost over a hundred dollars, which is pretty impressive for a pair of prison blues. Instantly, my thoughts take me to a pleasant place that I rarely am able to visit in prison. My mind floods with snapshots of my love affair and appreciation for clothes.

"SP come eat your breakfast before it gets cold!" My grandma called out to me. Knock. Knock. Knock. As I am dashing through the kitchen someone is at the back door. It's Corey, my best friend, who stands at six feet one inch, has a dark complexion and whose tiny teeth beam as he gives me a sly grin. He has two pair of jeans in his hands. "Ay, I need you to tell me which pair of these has doo-doo," he demands. We head up to my room where I have scattered around a few clothes myself trying to figure out the same issue as he. I leave him to fit his jeans in my room while I go into my closet and tear through shoe boxes. The front door screeches open then slams shut, dashing footsteps make their way up the stairs and stop in front of my bedroom door, and in bursts Annaroo. She is five-foot seven, half black, half Native American, has long Hawaiian Silky hair, and an attitude that just does not care. Whatever comes to her mind flies from her mouth and she'll think about apologizing later. Now that both of my neighbors are standing in my room I am almost certain that we're going to be late for school. "Hey boo, Hi Corey. What the hell is taking y'all so damn long?" she harks. "I'm ready but Corey stepped in doo-doo this morning," I say trying to shift the blame totally on Corey. This same song and dance is repeated at least 3 times a week. "Alright y'all come get your breakfast," Grandma yells up. She saves us from one of Annaroo's spirited rants. We begin to head down when

Corey yells, "Ay check my pants for doo-doo!" Anna checks the back of his pants to make sure they are adjusted on his hips just right, so that the appearance of a bulge is eliminated and doesn't look like he's hauling around a sack in the back of his pants.

"Dominick can you bring our plates outside on the porch?" Annaroo requested, and my youngest brother obliges. We don't want to sit in the kitchen because the scent of food will permeate our clothes and we'll smell of pancakes and sausage all day instead of Very Sexy, Chrome, and Joop. We're finally ready to go to school and as we we're collecting our book bags and heading toward the door, Grandma yells, "You all looks very nice but I wish ya' mommas wouldn't buy you all of those nice clothes because people are going to talk bad about you when you don't have them anymore." Naively it goes right over our heads. "Grandma is trippin'!" Corey says and we laugh right on out the door.

What started out as a teenage fad turned into a lifestyle of trend chasing for the three of us. Although as adults we led three very distinct lives, it's a commonality that bonds us. I'm not sure where their story begins but mine starts in the classroom.

I was in my favorite teacher's class long after school had let out. She was the most respected and rigorous teacher at my school. She stands about five feet even, has tiny black locked hair that is always pulled back, golden framed glasses, and she has amazingly perfect white teeth that are always accompanied by pleasant breath. She's one of the few healthy in-shape teachers at school. She complimented me on how I, along with some other students, often dress well, then she tells me how she read some studies that said, "The better students dress the better they perform in school," and, like a dummy I accredited my earned A's in her class to the way I dressed instead of to my diligent hard work. She left me with this, "If you look good, you'll feel good and when you feel good you'll do good…You'll do well. Good is something you taste. Remember this!" Because I held her in such high regard her advice always had more weight than others and from that moment on, I began dressing for success and not for fun.

I remember my first experience with the "High end." Being in the midst of bustling women who reeked of strong perfume similar to that of a grandma made my nose sizzle. I just wanted to get a bottle of Paradise, a new fragrance by Estee Lauder as a Mother's Day gift and get out of there. Making my exit I passed through the men's section into a Blvgari BLV display. It was enticing. It oozed, "T-r-y m-e, s-m-e-l-l, m-e, b-u-y m-e." Knowing that I couldn't afford anything Blvgari had to offer me I thought maybe, I could smell what that would feel like, so I smelled it. It took me on a trip; I was no longer standing inside of Neiman Marcus but in NYC co-mingling with my ideas of success. I had bought my first bottle without hesitation.

What started out as something that satisfied my pretentious hunger transgressed into a deeply rooted appreciation of artistic expression. The more I delved into this world of seemingly outrageous prices and expression that is hard to understand, I gained admiration. Since I couldn't afford these things, all I could do was to admire them. I admired them for their creativity, and their creator for their perseverance following their passion in such a misunderstood field. It was as if when I saw a designer's creation I wasn't looking at clothes at all but only the long tedious creative process that went into making something so simple as a shirt. I felt their struggle of becoming an established brand, because anyone who thinks you can wake up and make it in this fickle industry is mistaken. I felt admiration towards them for doing what they loved.

Now, as I look in awe at my own artistic expression through my pair of redesigned Prison Blues, I have just been inspired.

Jon Killoran

Earthquake Drills

"The doors to the world of the Wild Self are few but precious. If you have a deep scar, that is a door, if you have an old, old story, that is a door. If you love the sky and water so much you almost cannot bear it, that is a door. If you yearn for a deeper life, a full life, a sane life – that is a door."

– Dr. Clarissa Pinkola Estes

Doors. Lots of doors to the inner self. Got it. Doors to it. Doors away from it. Doors that initially lead away but come back after an illegal U-turn. There's a lot of friggin' doors, and some manic drive to find them like life's an earthquake drill.

Either that or we're all secretly locksmiths...

There are analogies involving doors, metaphors about doors that I don't get – the trick is to smile and nod thoughtfully – there are even anecdotes about doors. The Doors are probably in there somewhere.

Oh yeah, it all makes sense now...

If the inner-self is so full of doors then the least someone could do every once in a while is hawk a freakin' map. Otherwise I'm left standing confounded at the doggie-door of the inner-self, the revolving door of the inner-self, the elevator door of the inner-self.

There's no elevator, but somehow, there's still music...

To get this crap about doors, I need to be enlightened or a carpenter. If it makes sense then I've either gone crazy and broke myself or I gave up and am nodding thoughtfully.

Frankly, I'm sick of doors. My experience with doors is like the IRS: Knock, and no one answers. So unless someone advocates infesting the inner-self with termites, maybe I should look into getting rid of all these doors, and instead find some spaces big enough to do something in; good, bad, it's all baby steps...

Not that doors aren't great – you can shut them on foots and faces and bill collectors – but a door doesn't leave a lot of room for happiness.

Jon Killoran

Existentialism

(Stop, before you hurt yourself…)

Brandon Davila

Ink is Thicker...

My heart beats in rhythm with every stroke of my pen, the ink my blood, every word a sin. I spill my soul in everything I write, to you a piece of paper, to me, my life. The scenes I've seen at times make me wish I was born blind, so I write, my pen cries through dry eyes, blue tears rain through grey skies.

I don't write to ease my mind; I just know that this paper will always be here to listen. Listen as my pen whispers, collectin' thoughts, and keepin' secrets, lock and key it, tongue and cheek it, that is, unless the ink leaks it.

I'm curious on how much my pen weighs, or am I the only one strong enough to lift it, 'cause from my experience I'm the only one who knows they've been invented. I know that your intentions are good and you intended to write if you could but the time ain't good, you're so busy, and all I have is time, you're right, I only work full-time, attend 4 classes 6 nights a week, talk to troubled teens and feel guilty when I sleep. My bad, that is a little off subject, it is just that every time I see my pen I gotta touch it, I love it, without it I am nothin'. It's not game that flows through this ball point, it is my soul that stains each sheet. It's how I meet new people without the convenience of speech. It is as though every page is a piece of me.

My pen is my wing man, my counselor, and my friend. My pen allows me to send you my love and best wishes, hugs and kisses through x's and o's. My pen sends me home to you and only my pen knows where my love goes.

My pen is an extension of my mind, and in so many ways helped change my life, kept me up at night, and at times we fight, this thing just refused to move, other times it just goes, it flows prose, poems, music, and love letters. My pen has caused giggles, smiles and laughter, along with tears, both of joy and sorrow. I write tonight because tomorrow might not be promised, and while I might be missed, the might of my pen will still exist.

Francisco Hernandez

Light

Light
The light of life
Held tightly to my chest
What would be of my life if I let go

What brings me light?
The image of a bloodstained
Hand-hewn piece of lumber
Cut down from an orchard
Or a hillside forest
Roman steel driven into it
How many times

The suffering, cold steel cracking bones
Impacting warm flesh
Anguish, pain, cries
What I deserved

Innocent he cried out in pain
His pain for my sake
To bring me from the gloom of darkness,
And into the Father's radiant light.

kosal so

lightness of being

the perfect setting for a tragedy.
the humidity is just right.
a bridge overlooking the vista
and the migration of pollens.
desultory leaves and petals of platonic paradigms,
tolerant dandelions carried off to their purpose,
as we go about the routine of life.

pain is what you and i have in common.
i would gladly absorb the unspeakable
things you bury inside.
if i could convince you to think this through,
to find purpose and contentment in reality?

if you decide to blindly jump into the abyss,
i hope that it's cool and clear as the air
rushing to dry the tears away.
or as warm and peaceful, and quiet as the evening,
before someone finds you lying on the ground.

you're not old enough to drink,
but you're old enough to ponder this.
you're not old enough to drive,
but you're old enough to make this choice.
there's so much more to the business of living,
than that of the dead.
live.

HJ Walker

Lock Them Up
and Throw Away the Keys

Justice without mercy is the concept of warehousing. Without mercy is the idea of breaking the spirit, much like you would an unruly dog.

I am overwhelmed when I think about the justice system in America. Maybe at one time the founding fathers had the right concept, but personally that is pure speculation on my part. I am neither a history buff nor a constitutionalist. I am just assuming since the country was supposedly established upon Judeo-Christian values, there must have been a balance between justice and mercy in our early history. But then again with the hell fire and brimstone preaching maybe not.

When it comes to the justice system, I can really only speak from personal experiences. I admit that my own philosophical perceptions are in personal conflict. Maybe this is because I was reared in a hell fire and brimstone environment, with a tyrant father. For years I accepted the justice meted out toward me, and even believed that it was mercy just to be alive.

Like that whipped dog I accepted the beatings without understanding why, occasionally baring my teeth at the abuse. All my life I have been in trouble with the justice system in one fashion or another, not once did anyone bother to look to see if I had a splinter in my paw. It was always "lock him in a cage until the price for his sins have been paid in full."

Restorative Justice is a fresh philosophy to my tired old mind, but one that brings mercy to my soul. I am still overwhelmed by our justice system and its entrenchment by the good old boys. It has become a big business with powerful money. Powers that could care less about any philosophies of mercy and this class of whipped mutts.

Jon Killoran

More at 11

Love may be gentle, and love may be kind, but love also worries an awful lot.

Do you know I worry when a disaster occurs in your hometown? When there's one more victim wearing a face that looks like yours, carrying a name that reads like yours, or speaks with a voice that sounds like yours? Do you know I worry when floods and fires and winds and people threaten the things you love and hold dear?

Yes. I do.

Do you know I sometimes give in to the panic and fear, watching the news with the rest of the fear-addicted masses, hysteria on my mind? I'm drawn to the things I fear — even reminded to be afraid of things I don't fear — much like the insect to the bug zapper. Do you know I think of the gulf between us and wonder if you're safe on your side, if your abilities protect you from the ignorance and carelessness of others?

Yes. I do.

Do you know I worry when there's a robbery gone wrong? Do you know I worry when there's a robbery that's gone right? When the counts for the dead or missing or wounded grow by one? Do you know I worry about you being killed and eaten in a mini-zombie apocalypse, thanks to the bath-salt addicts? Would a gun or a dog protect you from the brain-cravings of the not-so-undead? Do you know I even worry when I hear that an Oregon woman was killed after being chased by a runaway train?

Yes. I do.

Do you know I worry when serial killers are on the loose and the crazies are making the world a little more interesting, if also scary? Do you know I worry about gas pedals getting stuck and everyone having to learn to defensively drive the hard way? What about deadly travel plans? Evil cauliflower outbreaks? Police standoffs and hostages taken? Insidious household appliances? Malfunctioning odor-eaters? Indolent doctors and clumsy surgeons leaving mystery items inside patients like a box of cracker-jacks? Coffee? What the hell's up with coffee? Insects hiding in your home? Capricious weather? Pharmaceuticals that increase your urge to gamble? Identity theft (especially if you have an identity worth stealing)? Spy programs and nuclear war? Wild animals at the zoo? What about escaped wild animals at the zoo? The terrors of hot-air balloons? Dangerous circus acts? The links between tequila and the lack of clothing? Over-friendly people? Asocial people? The things we don't know about car crashes that occur at less than 20 mph? Zeppelins made of lead, or even thermite? Anything covered by your insurance excepting accidents and acts of God?

Do you know I worry about those too?

Yes, believe it or not. I do.

I anxiously await not seeing a face I wish to see more than any other, or to not hear a name I long to hear – at 6, at 8, sometimes even at 10. I'm left hoping you're safe, and that one more dream hasn't become a statistic, that one more person hasn't slipped my reach even if they've slipped my grasp.

Yes. I do, and if you wonder what else I worry about, tune in for more at 11...

My Noninvasive Procedure

It isn't the comforting words from my mom or dad that give me reassurance. It isn't the caress from a lover that brings me pleasure. When it comes to doting devotion there is nothing that comes near the companionship it gives me. When I'm feeling somber, it beams me with gamma ray bursts of esteem. Addicted, because it supplies me with what no one else can. I have tried to leave vanity alone once or twice before only to flounder. When convinced enough that I am strong on my own, I've taken off the mask of superficiality. Uncomfortable, exposed, and as vulnerable as a white coat cub crouching in sandy brush. There is nothing to protect me. Every attack will penetrate straight through to the core of my feelings because there was nothing to deflect it.

Vanity has told me that no one and nothing would ever be as good to me as it has and I believe her. I often lie at her feet ashamed because I have relapsed to the only drug of my choice. Narcotics cause hallucinations, alcohol offers liquid courage but vanity's side affects are temporary confidence, false protection, pretentious assurance, and a dose of love that can get you higher than the Curiosity rover.

She is my compadre, confidant, and best friend. Even though she knows my every secret, my flaws and all, she never judges me, only helps me cover them up with her tools. I always believe vanity because she's never given me a reason not to, by carrying me such a long jagged distance with energy to spare, to doubt her wouldn't be right.

People have let me down and the world has muddied me up. She joins me in the bed at night, leads me to the closet and has me look into her glass eyes. It's not me she wants to focus on but all of the hanging helpers that are my backdrop. She tells me, "Pull it together SP! Don't you see what I see? Look at me! Here, use this facial cleanser to ease some of that worry in your face. Relax your forehead, wrinkles bring down your stock." Her ways are working. Her soothing voice says slowly, "That's much better. Your skin looks rejuvenated already. Moisturize with this Aloe Cucumber Shea butter mix. There you are my boy. Smile! Oh wait, grab the Carmex. Nobody likes a man with cracked lips, and yours my dear are perfect. You my dear are perfect. You need a small dollop of Missoni, you are never short any compliments when you smell so good. Turn around grab that black polo, those sand blasted jeans, orange belt, and your Bo Jacksons. Put them on and let me see you. Wow! If that's not the most handsome man that I've seen, I don't know what is. Are you telling me you don't see what I see? The man in front of me has charm and courage that will take him anywhere." I smile. The rejection I felt for her only moments before has dissipated. "Now run off, save face and put on a show, and when you step off of the world's stage remember you're the best to ever have done it."

I return from the closet into my room with all of vanity's tools infusing me with reinforcement. I again feel like greatness, even perfect, intoxicated because once again I have taken a long deep hit of vanity's love.

kosal so

playing god

my friend,
when he was five,
went into his mother's closet,
and put on her shoes and a dress.
when she caught him she asked "why?"
"i'm you mom!"

was it the absence of y's?
or too many x chromosomes
sliding to the left
stuck somewhere asking, "what am i?"

my hormones race for pretty pink,
but he wrestles being a boy
in a world of snarling werewolves
with sharp cutting eyes and judgmental teeth.
bite marks puncture his heart
maybe she should have stayed inside.

my younger brother too
was bullied by boys
who had not a clue who my sibling is.

do they even care to know all that he's accomplished?

why did some of the students during lunch throw food at him?
why did his teacher bash him?
why did the churchgoers say to me "fags go to hell!"

is hell where people go when they're different?
is hell where my friend will go to get god to listen?
is hell where my brother will no longer be judged?
if so, hell is where I hope to go.

kosal so

rimes of salt

i imagine my father coming home to an empty house.
what did the spirits of the house convey
about our frantic escape?
the same phantoms my mother prayed to for protection
and made offerings to when we first moved in,
failed to stop my father from bruising her face.

so when did my mother devise a plan to leave him
saving enough to purchase five plane tickets, clothes,
and a couple of suitcases,
then hurrying her children aboard a plane,
from columbus, ohio to long beach, california?

the unmade mattress, the old grimy furnace and neighbors,
what tale will they tell when they share stories
of a broken home?
i imagine the wind howling a song
as mournful leaves rustle into twilight,
weeping because my father is too stubborn
to cry for his wife and children?
i imagine the man finally breaking down,
when it all becomes too much to hold inside,
an ocean rushes from his eyes,
and he drowns.

kosal so

running water

the bright sky violet against the deep shadows,
ambient field of midsummer,
soon will become autumn.
fireflies twinkle like the milky way,
soon will flicker.
electricity on my skin,
hairs on the back of my neck,
fuzz on my arms and legs on the verge of flight.
nocturnal moon hovers like a lantern,
brisk and beautiful this awesome night.

at first a simple pace,
then the steps break into a run,
clovers curl into the ground.
twirling leaves rustle at my feet,
i am a rebel against the wind
howling at my face.
arms at my sides like no particular bird or plane
breathing heavily chasing the mist.

i should harvest my delight
before my mother call,
then i hear the sound of cars,
sirens in the distance,

telephone ringing and running water.

i'm staring out the window at the snow
in the kitchen washing dishes.

Jon Killoran

Say What?

There is power in our words. We know it when they're spoken, but we don't typically see it when they're written; not anymore. With taps of the fingers and a flick of the wrist, any thought can be crafted and sent into the world with less time and effort than it would take to actually speak that very thing.

We type and share nearly everything thanks to the ease and speed of doing so. Many of us are also willing to speak the majority of the things we type simply because of how insignificant the added effort to everyday conversations simple or shallow ideas is. Yet, we are aware of the energy required for any situation we deem important, and, whether spoken or written, we will select words to match not only the qualitative aspects of our efforts, but the quantitative as well. We may even be willing to handwrite short notes, simple lists, or the occasional postcard, but due to the intensive and tedious nature of handwriting, the number of thoughts and ideas we're willing to communicate in this format begins to shrink dramatically.

In short, the more effort required to share, the less likely we are to do so, regardless, perhaps, of the importance of our message.

Don't believe me? Participate in an exercise with me, will you? Select any thought, feeling, experience, or memory you possess. Think about it clearly, subvocalizing it in all its details, and approximate the time and effort that it takes to do this. Go ahead, I'll wait...

Type your idea, if possible, and try to be as accurate as you can. Approximate the time and effort for this as well.

Now, speak it as you thought it – every nuance, subtlety, inflection, and pause. Speak with the same speed and cadence that you thought it, again, approximating the time and energy required to do this.

With me still? Good. Now write down everything that you've spoken, noting once more the time and effort in doing this. Finally, for those that recall this particular skill, go back and rewrite everything you've just written in cursive. Note what it takes to do that too.

Did you find an increase in time? Energy? Was your thought as important to you in the end as it was in the beginning? More importantly, would you still share it under these conditions? What if this was the only way to share your thoughts?

This isn't to say that only slow and laborious methods of communication are valuable - we don't carve our words in stone – nor am I saying that a thought need survive this particular little exercise before you decide if it should be shared.

I am saying we, and the world at large by extension, would be better served if we just took a moment to think about the things we say. Just because it can be said doesn't mean it should be, and just because it is doesn't mean that it holds any inherent value, even when we're the ones that are saying it.

Whether or not we handwrite our every thought, we should at least be willing to consider if a particular notion means enough for us to do so. Especially since, for some, writing is the only means by which to communicate to the world at large.

So, what do you have to say?

Jon Killoran

Sayings That Shouldn't Make Sense

Whoever says "Money can't buy you happiness" has neither enough nor the ability to use it correctly.

Self-Respect is that thing that makes people boring.

It's better not to do something for someone when you can help them do it for themselves.

It's only cheating if you're caught, but, it'll always be lying.

Forgetting is the same as forgiving. Go ahead, try it.

Help someone in trouble and they'll just come to you the next time they're in trouble.

Anything written in a fortune cookie.

If coincidence is aligned with the Will of God, then you're probably trying to justify something you've already planned.

People are going to do whatever it is they're going to do whether they want to or not.

Loving your neighbor as yourself only counts if you actually like yourself. Else, ignore it…and them.

Reading any of these and thinking "That shouldn't make sense."

Jon Killoran

Staring is Always Creepy

Billy Collins once noticed poets at their windows, but it's really about the look—the catalyst that arises from the creative engines of the soul to fuel the mind and move the hand:

The lazy look of a poet with no destination, meandering, picking up jewels here and there like pearls from an oyster—food for body and mind.

The contemplative look of a poet writing a poem with no words, playing the goalie against the verse and prose that threaten to topple the moment—Zen-like whimsy mirroring the coffee: Good to the last drop.

The focused look of a poet with points of origin and end in mind, wondering how many letters does it take to move from Point A to Point Z as efficiently as possible—a path for the masses and others to follow and be inspired by.

The wry look of a poet who sees the humor in it all, wielding barbs both subtle and sharp, insults without malice, humor in meaning in humor such that Buckminster Fuller would be proud—steps implied and meaning, a treasure hunt.

The confused look of a poet who doesn't know why he's in the window in the first place, missing the point of the exercise, wondering at the philosophic wonders contained in the neighbor's fern and his own willingness to waterboard it in order to get them—the poet whose friends not everyone can see...

Okay, so maybe not everyone in the window is a poet, but, for those that are, it's all about the look.

SP

The Battle

Speeding down a Texas highway at eighty miles an hour and suddenly, a plastic Safeway bag starts whipping around the car. I panic. It temporarily impedes my view of the road. I take one hand off of the wheel and reach for the whirling bag. My control of the steering wheel is lost but I quickly regain control, Annalisa captures the bag. Two eighteen year olds continued traveling in silence, a hollering silence. It yells how bad that could have been, a major multi car pile-up, and surely us dead or gravely wounded.

This is one of many instances where what could have easily turned out to be a devastating event, misses me. At times, it is as if I am being spared, protected and groomed for an occasion that I am unaware of. I look at the people and places with whom I co-exist, to discover clues; to who I am what I am, and mostly, to see how I am perceived. This information is then cross referenced with how I view myself. The two matching up is a rarity and internal conflict ensues.

Jon Killoran

The Big Book of Cynical Philosophy

Aristotle's *De Anima*, Plato's *Republic*, Voltaire's *Candide*, Kant's *Critique of Pure Reason*, Freud's unhealthy obsession with mothers, and William James' *Pragmatism*; all of them, things you've never heard of and wouldn't understand if you had.

Certainly no one else confuses Plato with a toy, clay product, or thinks that Voltaire is an electrical term. The world, even such as it is, has still managed to bear witness to sock puppets of higher IQ — they don't need to cram all night just to order lunch, or guess at their own name.

Then again, neither do they think Kant is a contraction, or that his categorical imperative has anything to do with the question selection process for Jeopardy, since, as sock puppets, they don't think at all.

At least you have something in common...

It's not like you're completely unlikable though — aside from the fact that the Plague has more Facebook friends than you — but maybe you should strongly consider why you get a fifth of whiskey and a straight razor every year for Christmas.

So, anything you read hereafter, albeit slowly and aloud, you're not going to understand any more than when the Tooth Fairy stopped paying you for your teeth at the age of 21, unless, someone were to take pity on you and break out the crayons for some helpful diagrams.

While you're blithely shoving crayons in your nose and wondering why your parents cry every time they look at you, the rest of us will have a blast at your considerable expense; a target rich environment of one.

See, everyone important wins…

Thus said, I'd like to dedicate this work to you, the reader: Without your contributions, the world is a better place.

Enjoy the bright colors and pretty words…

On God: Don't worry, He doesn't believe in you either

On Suicide: Always an option, but, for some it's mandatory

On Marriage: Don't

On Children: See Marriage

On Love: Who hates themselves enough to love you?

On Paranoia: Assume these walls could talk…about you…

On Life: Overrated

On Comedy: The only joke is you

On Nihilism: Life is meaningless…

On Existentialism: …or is it? Hint: See Nihilism

On Pets: The highest form of sentient life that will ever be happy to see you

On Truth: Assume you can't handle it, we do

On Politics: Where both sides agree you're an idiot

On Occupation: No one will pay you to go away

On Philosophy: Things you don't understand in words you'll never use

On Gambling: Your existence is a gamble

On Right and Wrong: You're incapable of one…guess which…

On Friendship: Even the imaginary ones don't like you

On Nature vs. Nurture: Either way you're screwed

On Deceit: You're an intelligent, thoughtful, creative human being, and I respect you highly

On the value of Life: Pick a number, then mock yourself

On Pragmatism: Your existence is an affront to it

On Education: A learning curve isn't supposed to be flat

On Family: The most familiar group of people to ever dislike you

On Hope: Stop, please. You're only embarrassing yourself when you do that

This is the end; you can quit moving your lips and pretending to read.

kosal so

which god?

he would beat my mom until blood spilled,
her black and blue face always gives me chills.

balling my fist to up rise,
but i'm too little to defy.

all i could do was turn off lights,
then wait for morning to rescue night.

i shut my eyes and purged my ears,
but her screams won't silent and tears won't veer.

open my eyes only to find,
we're still trapped in the same place.

the only comfort is each other's embrace,
and the warmth of a mother's battered face.

clinging to one another confused and bruised
dad is in the kitchen searching for his tool.

i wonder if it will hurt when the blade pierces through?
what on earth is a child supposed to do?

which god am i supposed to pray to?

Regrets

Charles C. Hammond II

Home Town

September 8, 2014

I awake many times: arms outstretched reaching toward the ever-elusive tangibility of a past life that I shattered into far too many pieces to be able to reassemble. Through the haze of deteriorated memories, I can vaguely recall a place that I once called home. As I wipe the sleep from my eyes, I can scarcely make out the outline of home through the invading reality of the oncoming day that inevitably overshadows the serenity of it. To attempt to reconstruct what was lost would utterly fail, no matter how it was sought after, and though there are far too many pieces missing for it to ever be complete again, the desire never fades.

There is a faint scent on the fringes of my senses that beckons me to return, to find my way back, to reinsert myself back into the collective. However, after two decades I am uncertain of how. Will I be a relic of a happily forgotten time? I seem to be on a pathway to the unknown to renovate what cannot be rebuilt.

It's funny; I spent my childhood wanting nothing more than to sever my ties that bound me to a town where everyone knows your name, where you live, who to call when you misbehave. Now, my dream and desires are about returning to be a part of that small town where everyone knows your name, where you live, and that even though you were someone known for doing some pretty stupid things in your youth, that you are once again home; that the town was somehow whole again due to my return. With enthusiasm I will traverse whatever comes my way for I have to know, I have to see, I have to rediscover who and what I am to be.

Regretfully, in many ways I received exactly what I asked for. I escaped, but the grass is never as green as the grass under your feet to begin with, and is never the same when reality brings your perspective into true focus and you return once again to recapture youthful innocence that is forever changed. The serenity and bliss of the ignorance that seemed to be such a hindrance no longer seems to be all that bad of an innocence. Unfortunately, once "Pandora's Box" is opened it can never be contained. Regardless, I will try with all that I possess. I will, once again, find home even if it has changed, even if it is gone.

Benjamin James Hall

10 p.m. Endless Climb

The tier dark and empty as an asylum's graveyard shift.
Besieged beneath dim light, sown under,
Unable to stop welling tears,
Leaking from windows of the soul.

Thirteen protracted years clawing, scratching, climbing
From a horrible rotting cavity
Just to have hate's hands drag me back down.
Clinging desperately to sides without footholds
Filthy mud sliding between futile fingers.

Unfilled, vacant, parched, run dry
Longing desperately to rise above this prison and its politics.
Fighting persistently but so very fatigued
Seducing voices echo in whispers, urging momentarily to rest.
A sleep of a definite, which I know I'll not awaken.

Would that this heart be arctic again
Fallow ground, barren and callous.
Why now must it feel so acutely?
A soul laid upon the tracks, packed down and silenced,
Holding a lifeline and fighting solid yet gaining zero ground

Kicking away a sea of grasping fingers off my ankles.

But one pair of hands remains
Clenched like the seize of heroin
Unable to beat this fiend, knowing what must be done.
I've got to kill this man!
Climbing down to do the hands in, horrified,
The prisoner looks into his own eyes, grasping his own hands.

Phillip

California Son

Fun?
When I was young
You needed a knife
Or a gun

Sun, Surf?
You hold your ground
You fight for turf

Never realized this was wrong
Never thought I'd live this long

Didn't think my childhood was bad
It seemed normal and yet so sad

I'm still alive and I am glad
Looking back on my life makes
Me mad,
I'm a California son

James M. Anderson

Fertility

I am a seed
Caught in the wind
Drifting…
With absolutely nowhere to land.
My life is getting shorter now.
I harbor thoughts of fertility
Longing, yearning to find a home.
But there is nowhere to go.
Nowhere…
Because the wind carries
An element of lost time,
Time that can't be retrieved.
Nor re-lived.

So I drift,
I wander,
I ride the wind…
Because only the wind
Can dictate where I roam.
And while I do…
I wonder.
I think constantly
Of what could have been.
A career, a family

Cherished memories that never fade.
The beautiful intricacies of life fulfilled
Had I not traveled the path I made.

I am but a seed.
Caught in the wind,
Drifting.
Soaring high
And sometimes low.
My life continuing to shorten
Despite my eagerness to finally grow.
As I drift…
I scream blaspheme to the wind
With a long, drawn-out, exhale.

James M. Anderson

From the Start

When I was born,
You hid in the shadows
Watching me,
Stalking me intently as my
Mother held me softly
Within her arms.
She beamed in the
Aftermath of childbirth,
Exhausted, yet gazing
At me lovingly with pride.
Her fingers ran through my
Soft wisps of blond hair,
Thankful for a healthy baby boy.
You were there too,
Waiting furiously with impatience.

Your aim?
To claim me as your own,
To rob me of my sanity
My sense of self worth,
And to make instability
My middle name.
You wanted a victim,
And you found me.

When I slept…
You pounced on me,
Smothering me with the
Vile inadequacy of self loathing
And dire undefeatable depression.

As I grew older,
You fought hard to keep me down.
For every positive I'd hear,
You'd counter it by whispering
A hundred negatives in my ear.
A hundred and one to be exact.
You whispered them so convincingly
That I couldn't help but believe you.

I tried not to,
But I failed.

You don't have a voice,
But I'd hear you.
And I hated it.
You don't have a face,
But in my own reflection
I can see clearly the
Masterpiece you've carved,
And I hate it too.
Your name……?
Depression.
When I'm at my lowest,

I can feel you.
I hate you,
Because I'm your victim.

Benjamin James Hall

Listen!

I can hear the uncontrolled sobs behind me, each one piercing my heart with the force of a hammered spike. My mind treks back to those words we all hear as children repetitiously: *Pay Attention! Listen!* *"You never listen,"* my dad yells, and curses at me. He is angry because strangers brought me home. The couple hit me with their car; I had run out in the street without looking both ways. I didn't pay attention.

Pay attention! "It's just a bunch of nonsense," says Mr. O'Connell, my fifth grade teacher. "Go clean the blood off your face. You just don't listen boy, it's disgusting."

Sitting in MacClaren's juvenile youth authority lockup at sixteen, Mo Popov, the cottage counselor, screams inches from my face, "So you think you're a tough guy, huh?" I roll my eyes and he responds sharply with, "Roll your eyes all you want but you'd better listen close and pay attention good because I'm going to tell you your future, tough guy. You will graduate this MacClaren School for boys and make it to the Oregon State Correctional Institution. From there you'll finally make it to the big time baby, Oregon State Penitentiary. And when you're there in your little cesspool life you'll remember my words." This dude doesn't know what he's talking about, I'm thinking. Not many years later, sitting in Oregon State Correctional Institution's Segregation unit, what we call the hole, my head is in a toilet with pumped-out water. Tommy is yelling down the line in search of tobacco smuggled in concealed in a dark and most offensive place. Momentarily, Mo's words concerning my cesspool life enter my mind, but I'm still not listening.

Standing in the street barely six months out of prison, my mother hugs my motionless body, as I stare blankly through welling tears, ignoring my conscience. Listen to me son, my mother pleads. I love you! I know your salvation was real. She grabs my shoulders begging me not to go. I hear her words, but I'm not listening. I'm not paying any attention. I climb into my stolen Mazda 626 and drive away. Listen! PAY ATTENTION!

For the first time in, I can't even remember when my dad is hugging me, it feels awkward. "I love you son," he says as I open the front door. "Listen to me, my son," my dad's eyes are pleading with me, but in my mind my feet are already moving out the front door and into the street. Listen, pay attention.

The judge's voice and the cries behind me in the court room bring me back to reality as the judge sentences me to 22 and a half years in prison. I am listening now but mostly to my mother's sobs.

kosal so

sandcastles

inhale,
then exhale,
the rues,
of life's sonic tides.

the ocean's undulant breath
such a quiet gale.
the ocean breathes,
exhaling waves of bubbles
between my toes.

sand clings onto my feet
as i walk across the shore,
where sediments have remained.

who am i to intrude
and leave my tracks?
i will only live briefly
if i even exist at all.

the ocean agrees,
wave after wave crashes,
fierce beautiful soft foam
sent to retrieve my footprints.

they disappear.

inhale,
then exhale,
the seconds,
minutes, hours,
days, weeks,
years.

i will be no more.
no one will know i was ever here,
but the ocean will go on,
& time,
time will go on,
counting without me.

kosal so

held reservoir

i am at a loss for language,
searching for metaphor.

if i could just hold you
and not say a word,
i would hold you in a quiet reservoir.

if only i could conjure a comparison,
or metamorphose into a sponge
to soak up the tiny body of water.

i cry and heave
because i don't know the words to restore
you to your held offspring home.

what could i possibly say?

i will firmly hold you in cupped hands,
and wait.

rivers will turn to oceans
from tears not persuaded to fall.

i will simply lie down
to die with you.

James M. Anderson

Thunder and Rain

Four walls of concrete and stone,
Impenetrable to everything but the mind.
Years of isolation and self doubt,
Making reality seemingly impossible to find.
Raging rivers of regret and remorse,
Water levels rising through punishment and shame.
Caught in the eye of a strengthening storm,
While searching frantically through the thunder and rain.

A growing sense of hopelessness,
Disappointments outpacing the tunnel's light.
A never ending cycle of consistent misery,
As though I'm drowning in the regrets of this life.
Why endure and shoulder these conditions,
Continuously struggle with so little to gain.
What reasons could you possibly give?
To encourage pushing on through the thunder and rain.

Trying to believe that rehabilitation matters,
Despite years of the systems deceiving illusions.
Sunless skies, strained and swollen eyes,
Fooled by false promises and inner confusion.
5,088 days stranded,
Hunkered down and humbled by memories ingrained.

A desperate search for fleeting forgiveness,
Despite each step forward being slumbered in pain.

Lost in the winds of a runaway storm,
Headed in a directionless tailspin of sorrow.
Loneliness, emptiness and heartache,
Rough enough today, I can't imagine tomorrow.
No one understands the ironies faced,
Or the inner battles I fight in vain.
So difficult to move beyond my past,
When it's littered with stains I can't explain.

Seclusion a foregone conclusion,
Absentmindedness a way to medicate the mind.
An unshaven and disheveled appearance,
Walking these halls as though I'm blind.
Muffled sobs heard throughout the night,
Silence only briefly contained.
All these tears shed in loneliness,
Only adding to the thunder and rain.

James M. Anderson

Time

I looked at my watch today. I looked at it half expecting for the first time to understand what time really means and how it corresponds with the five thousand, three hundred and eighty one days that I've been imprisoned.

One hundred twenty nine thousand, one hundred and forty four hours spent wondering what amount of time will ever truly make up for my wrongs and how I can take it upon myself to make seemingly impossible amends.

Seven million, seven hundred forty eight thousand, and six hundred and forty minutes alone in regretful personal reflection. Reflection that only shows me time and time again that remorse never fades, never forgets, and never frees me from the realization that time can never be relived. Time? Time is the magnifying glass to life's regrets, never to be ignored.

Four hundred sixty four million, nine hundred eighteen thousand, and four hundred seconds that I've sat here wishing I could go back and change a mere sixty minutes of my youth.

When I looked at my watch today, I did so desperately hoping that in those tiny, melodically intricate hands of seconds, minutes, and hours I'd see for the first time a glimpse of light at the end of this tunnel.

But what I saw, and what made me lower my head with tightly clinched eyelids was that, like prison, a watch is only there to remind you of where you're at in that exact moment.

There's no going back, no possibilities or openings for the heart-broken and humble apology that I've ached to give since I was 17 years old.

I see now that time is not only my prison; it's also the measurement of life's mountainous mistakes. Mistakes that eventually pile up and overcome us as inevitable landslides of regret and remorse. My watch blinds me with its truth, yet tomorrow I'll surely look again.

Nestor Diaz-Miller

Where Were You Last Night?

Where were you last night? I needed you and you were nowhere to be found. You told me that no matter what I could trust you and ask for help whenever I needed to. Even when you broke up with me, I still had hopes for a better tomorrow. Even while you shattered my fragile heart into pieces, I still loved you. While we were saying our good-byes, I was trying to tell you something but couldn't. I was trying to tell you I was pregnant with our child. I was under so much pressure. I was confused and emotional, to say the very least. Most of all I was scared and I had no idea how to break the news to you. We were still so young and I didn't know if we were both ready to be parents. But, I was willing to take that step with you and you alone.

Days turned into weeks of anticipation, just waiting for you to reach out to me. I just wanted you to take me back. Whatever I did to make you upset with me, I knew I could change. I still remember all those late nights sleeping alone in bed with my phone in hand waiting for it to show your picture once more. On one of those late nights filled with tears and heartache, I felt the pain inside of me growing larger. I knew something was wrong. I was frozen in place with my phone in hand hoping the pain would dissipate. I was just about to call you when it all started. The agonizing pain grew with each moment that ticked away on the clock. I panicked and started to call your phone over and over again. All my efforts came to no avail. I was all alone.

I struggled to get to the car. I knew I had to get to the hospital as soon as I could. I couldn't wait any longer. Tears blurred my vision as I drove, wincing in pain I cried out for you. The crying grew louder with each mile that passed. Walking through the sliding door of the emergency room, I was immediately met by a couple of nurses. They knew I was in dire need of help. My sobbing turned to weeping as I began to realize the inevitable was coming to be our sad truth. During this all I could think of was your hands holding mine, you whispering in my ear telling me everything was going to be alright. I just wanted your reassurance that we were going to get through this together.

But, still you were nowhere to be found. I kept hoping this was all just a scare and that everything was normal, but somewhere in the back of my mind I knew the harsh reality was coming. When all the nurses were done with me and the doctor came in clipboard in hand, time slowed to a halt, my breathing ceased, and my heart stopped. The sound of the door closing behind him sent chills down the soul of my spine. Then he would speak the words I will never forget: "I'm so sorry, miss. We did everything we could, but we were too late. Is there anyone we can contact for you?"

That was our child. I had already imagined the white picket fenced-in yard. I had already thought about you playing in the grass together as father and child. I even pictured the first day of school and how overprotective you would be at the bus stop telling the driver to take extra care today. We were going to be a family. We were going to live our happily ever after together. And for once in my life something was going to be worth living for.

Now that dream has all but faded into the distance. All of those guarded emotions have dissipated and left my heart for good. Now I feel the emptiness inside of me, not only in my stomach but in my chest as well. A piece of my heart has been ripped away. I'm not sure if I can bear to live anymore. This is too much. It's overwhelming me and engulfing my mind with thoughts that I can no longer tolerate. I don't know what to do. I don't know if I will ever recover from this. I don't believe in God, but today I might have to make an exception and pray for help.

Well, I am home now. And still no answer from your cell phone. I suppose I'll try to fall asleep to the early morning news. Here we go, there is the seven day forecast, now what? "BREAKING NEWS! Three suspects apprehended and arrested for their involvement in a home invasion gone wrong. They will be charged with murder." What the hell? Oh my God…. That's your name. That's your picture as a mug shot. Oh, please! Please, no! Why you? Please, not today of all days. I didn't think this day could possibly get any worse, but it just did. Now I have lost both the people I have ever loved in one fell swoop. As the tears leave my eyes, they drop like bullets piercing the front of my shirt. I am in utter disbelief. I am confused beyond comparison.

But, now I know where you were last night.

Nestor Diaz-Miller

Whisper to a Roar

There seems to be a constant irritating noise that clutters my mind. At times, it sounds like a faint whisper from a distance, but then all of a sudden it unexpectedly takes the shape of a loud roar with attention-seeking purposes.

I believe it to be something like an addiction. In a peculiar sort of way, I think you have become my foreign forbidden substance. My piece of fruit from the tree of life, never to be mingled with, but much like any other forbidden substance, it had started harmless and of perceived good intentions, yet it morphed into an almost all-out binge of uncontrollable proportions. There seems to be no sense of moderation at all. The whisper to a roar once more. Calling to me to answer the sound.

I use my newfound addiction to attempt the covering of holes within my tempted soul, or to at least make efforts to fill them with more regrets, resentment, and sorrow.

I use the Band-Aid to cover the much-needed stitch job. I spend so much time taking on everyone else's broken hopes that my own hopes have all but evaporated into thin air. My young self is feeling as breakable as an old brittle tree fearing the next major windstorm. My old soul starting to take its form on my once welcoming exterior. My cheerful spirit feeling calloused and worn to the core.

This noise I fight. This racket has rattled me. These voices are overlapping in my mind. My emotions have entangled themselves and I can't tell reality from fiction anymore. These strange feelings of old have once again taken root in the garden of my mental capacity. They have pushed themselves to the forefront of my mind and have made a new dwelling place there. My consciousness has receded from shouting distance. I can no longer decipher the code between what is real and what is shrapnel of my old fragmented heart. The only right answer I can muster is to indulge in my addiction once more. You somehow hold the key to unlock all the answers that I long ago locked away and you share the remedy to my starving soul. I am thinking of you once more when I know that I shouldn't. Here it comes again: the whisper to a roar.

Will there be a day when I can silence the lion? With the ever-passing collection of heartbeats, I can only expect more adversity before the thrill of victory can ease my soul.

This new conquest shall end all remnants of doubt. I will no longer allow myself to indulge solely for the sake of indulgence. I will awaken from the ruins and I will quiet the storm of sorrows.

I will find a way to mute all that deafens. I will find the solution to turn the lion's roar to a faint, distant, and small whisper once again. I shall regain the power over my stronghold. Now the roar to a whisper.

James M. Anderson

Who Would Have Known?

Age 17
Who would have known?
All his calls home
Would be dialed from a prison phone.
His head bowed
Phone held tightly against his ear,
Fingertips catching tears
As his mother swears that she'll be here…
Or there,
She'll always be there to give him hope,
Through birthdays, visits, and random letters
She's there to help him cope.

Age 25
He's still trying to figure out this prison life,
But it's hard to mentally focus
When it's filled with misery and strife.
He tries to keep it light,
Tries to keep it simple day by day,
Always looking for the sunshine
And a means to chase the rains away.
But the struggle with shame still stays,
As seems to be the story of his life,
Prison now the punishment

From the standpoint that his wrongs outweigh his rights.
And in the silence of the midnight nights,
As his conscience comes calling for a fight,
He agonizes over the realization
That it's his own hands that took a life.
A coward is the sight
As he sees the mental reflection in the mirror,
Eyes pleading for forgiveness
But the walls in prison never hear.
So in agony he screams out that he's sorry
He screams out loud again and again,
Hoping that he'll somehow come to terms
With the horrible scars of sin.

Age 32
Who would have known?
All his calls home
Still being dialed from a prison phone.
His head bowed,
Phone still held tightly against his ear,
Fingertips still catching tears
As his mother swears that she'll be here…
Or there,
She'll always be there to give him hope.
Through birthdays, visits, and random letters,
She's there to help him cope.

Acknowledgments

The Penned Thoughts writers are forever grateful to the many people and organizations who have helped bring this book to life and/or have supported us in other ways since we began.

Chemeketa Community College has sponsored this group for years, thanks to the founding efforts of Nancy Green, the now retired executive director of corrections education. We appreciate the continued support from her successor, Jon Tucker. Other current and past Chemeketa encouragers include Julie Huckestein, Jim Eustrom, David Hallett, Don Brase, Rebecca Hillyer, Nancy Duncan, Peggy Greene, Jamie Wenigmann, Nancy Howard, Richard Shirer, Sandra Aguinaga, Marilee Moore, and Betsy Simpkins.

Our deepest thanks go out to the Chemeketa Press staff who made this project possible: Steve Richardson, Brian Mosher, Ronald Cox, and Stephanie Lenox.

The Oregon State Penitentiary chaplains have graciously provided the Chapel Library for our class and events over the years. Kelly Raths, Richard Torres, and Phil Holbrook gave us the space early on in the group's life. We have since enjoyed continued support from chaplains Larry Bowen, Dennis Stahlnecker, Karuna Thompson, and Avrohom Perlstein.

In addition, none of our work would be possible without the support of Oregon State Penitentiary security and activities staff. Special thanks go out to Mike Yoder, Amy Pinkley-Wernz, Carla Padilla, Ray Austin, Michelle Dodson, Crystal Archdeacon, Jeff Premo, Dawnell Meyer, Jaime Rodriguez, Patrice Lans, Courtney McFadden, Steve Finster, Robin Burch, Bill Marion, David Wilson, and Tonya Gushard.

We owe a debt of gratitude for a generous donation from the Metro West Women's Club.

Helena Longton, a steadfast supporter and blessing for many years, has provided more assistance than we could possibly list here.

Colin Stapp is another long-time supporter who deserves special recognition for his technical expertise and moral support.

We are also grateful to Oregon House Rep. Paul Evans, Sister Helen Prejean, Shaul Cohen, the Lane Literary Guild, Tricia Hedin, Soapbox Poetry, Maggie Powers, Heather Powell, Craig Lancaster, Matt Love, Naseem Rakha, Tammy Jabin, Jill Rupert, Stacey Astill, Lauren Kessler, Tobi Jacobi, Patrick Berry, Kimberly Drake, Laura Rogers, Wendy Wolters Hinshaw, Cory Holding, Phyllis Hastings, Sam Temple, Tina Temple, Carole Coon, Marlene Pisha, Griffin Mc-Cormack, Katie Dwyer, Jeri Dwyer, Kathryn Dysart, Sally Driver, Cindy Sparks, Erin Strange, Melissa Tietz Ruge, Megan Torres, Kehala Hervey, Phoebe Petersen, Madeline Bailey, Chris Miller, Megan LaFollett, Steve Slemenda, Josh Cain, Trevor Walraven, Karen Cain, Carrie Zumbrum, Lauren L. Zavrel, Terry Stein, Janet Narum, Lani Sykes, Kelly Davidson, and others who have read our work, joined us for readings, written with us, and fed our spirits.

Author Biographies

James M. Anderson

As one of the original members of the Penned Thoughts writers' group I'd like to show my appreciation and give thanks for the countless hours that Michele spent helping us to fine-tune our craft. This book is proof that amazing things happen when poeple discover their voices as writers and find new ways to express the many complexities of life. Especially for those of us incarcerated. My hope is that through our words the reader will see clearly that prisoners are more than the sum of their mistakes; we're more than who we were on our worst day.

I may have come to prison as a 17-year-old, first-time offender, but I'm blessed and thankful for the opportunity to leave prison one day as a published writer and college graduate. I will use these blessings for the rest of my life to give credence to the fact that education is imperative when it comes to changing lives for the better.

Brandon Davila

My first memory of writing something comes from the 9th or 10th grade when I wrote a poem about Tupac right after he was killed. I remember reading it during a creative writing class and the reaction I received showed me that my pen could evoke emotion, both from the audience and myself, and it didn't hurt that I was pretty good at it. From there I started writing non-stop, including writing songs for a rap group that I was in (shout out to the B.N.$ Click), my delivery

239

was horrible, but my lyrics were off the hook leading me to "Ghost Writing," where I write and someone else raps it.

I write because I love making people smile and laugh, I love making people think, and I love that my words can impact change and break down barriers. I write because I can cry through this ink, I can make sense of my life, my past, my future, and my present. If freedom is a piece of mind, then my pen is the key to my deepest thoughts. In the end I write because I was born with a gift and I want to share my everything, give my all to those who have done the same for me.

Being a member of Penned Thoughts is AMAZING. It is more than a writer's group. It is a close knit pack of friends, it is a therapy session, it is a group of talented individuals sharing their fears, dreams, love, hurt, and secrets not to just each other, but to the world.

I am not defined by my cell number or my SID. I am defined by my actions, my hard work, and each and every word that leaks out of this ball point. I am a son, a brother, a friend, I am a student and a teacher, I am a writer, but most of all I am a man with his whole life ahead of him and up is the only way I am going! I am blessed to have been chosen not just to be a part of this book, but to be chosen to be a part, a piece in the puzzle that is P.T.G! I will continue to pen my thoughts, most likely in some kind of rhyming scheme (sorry, Michele), and I will NEVER shy away from doing me! Thank YOU for your support! Take care and God Bless!

LO1VE
Brandon Davila

Nestor David Diaz-Miller

I never really thought of myself as a writer when I was younger, but over time I've realized that writing has always been a type of escape from the reality I lived through. A way to release the pain, a way to heal, and a way move forward. I have always had a way with words, but I never imagined myself sharing my work to the public. But, here I am, ready to share myself through my words. Being a writer has always impacted my life in a positive way. I remember my freshman year of high school. I had an English teacher who would let me write stories as a way to get extra credit to help get my grades up. She was always encouraging me to be a writer, but I never really pursued it until later in life.

Several years later after I was incarcerated I was asked to take part in a writing seminar. After having a prompt on how we had ever been harmed, I wrote a piece about my history and shared it in my small group. Then I was politely forced to share that piece of writing. Afterwards the entire room expressed to me how thankful they were that I shared. It was then that I knew I needed to devote myself to writing. At the conclusion of that seminar, I was approached by a professor named Michele McCormack. She told me how much she enjoyed hearing my writing and that she would like to have me in her Penned Thoughts writers' group.

Now it's been almost five years later and I have been a member of the Penned Thoughts Group (PTG) ever since. I feel blessed to have been a part of PTG, and I look forward to continuing my work within the group for a long time. I'd like to express my sincerest gratitude to all my friends and family who have always supported me, to my freshman English teacher, to Professor McCormack, and lastly I'd like to thank the Father above for giving me the gift with words.

Benjamin James Hall

I have been in prison for 18 years and the weariness of this often apathetic environment has sometimes caused my life to feel polluted. Learning the practice of writing has been a way to purge that pollution from my life. Being a part of Penned Thoughts writing group has often been a lifeline to me in the midst of a prison that is an ocean of complexities. I think one of the most powerful things we possess is narrative, everyone has a context and we truly cheat ourselves when we don't take the time to learn the context of others. It is a blessing to hear the writing of the men around me as they tell their stories with all the force of creativity.

I recently read about a writer who lives in Iraq, he spoke about the difficult task of trying to write in the center of a violent city where he constantly thought about death coming at any moment. He went on to say that hopelessness is the limit and the beginning of a new kind of hope; and that hopelessness makes possible new hope. For me this captures the magic of writing. We can put our voice on paper in a creative way that is unique yet connects to others on the universal things all of us experience in life within our own context. People often say to me "I just can't write. I'm not good at it," but I believe everyone can write and if it is simply about your life, or your thoughts, then it is of value and someone wants to hear your voice.

I love writing. Through writing I have transcended these walls, walls that attempted to leave me here in the silence but writing gave me a new freedom inside, a fortress that even the hammer of time cannot penetrate. I am so thankful to God and the men and woman who gave me this opportunity to share my voice with the world outside these prison walls.

Charles C. Hammond II

When I was a freshman in high school, I had my first experience with creative writing. I was in a literature and writing class and our teacher asked us to write a piece that was descriptive, as well as creative. It took just a moment for me to come up with a subject. I had remembered a story that I saw once in a cartoon; it was about Ferdinand the Bull. In the assignment, I discovered my ability to describe what I saw with a great amount of detail. My teacher took me aside and told me that I should continue to write, but being the rebellious teenager that I was, I chose to do otherwise.

It wasn't until I came to prison that I really began to re-explore my ability to write. I have found that as I have grown, so has my ability to be descriptive. Now, I write to help others to share in my experiences, strengths, and hopes for the future. I attempt to elicit an emotional response that one has experienced in their own life to relate to what I feel at the moment.

The Penned Thoughts group has given me the opportunity to grow in ways that I never would have been able to without it. It is not only the platform that it provides to share my work, but it is the feedback that we give to one another that helps us to grow, to stretch, to see from perspectives that we would not have seen elsewhere. I also think that our writing group helps others to see that those that are incarcerated are not lost to their crimes, but that we can and do flourish when shown that we have the potential to be more, and that what we have to share is valuable. Maybe in some small way, what we share can change perceptions in a way that could change worldviews of who and what we are.

What is most important to me, other than my faith in God, is to cultivate potential anywhere that it may be exhibited. It is in that cultivation that purpose in life is most often found. It is in that realization of one's potential that the world can be changed.

Francisco Hernandez

I began writing at the age of twenty-one as a way to deal with a very difficult time in my life. In the midst of that dark time I found comfort, hope, and light in my writing. Many years later I was involved in a few writing workshops that helped me heal from some traumatic events in my life, specifically the murder of one of my friends. This gave me the realization of the tremendous healing powers of writing.

I joined the Penned Thoughts Group (PTG) in 2013, and since then it has been a place of refuge, joy, healing and friendship. This environment has given me the ability to grow in confidence as a writer and artist. In the group no one is criticized for their writing, we just listen and give positive feedback. Penned Thoughts has been a light to this prison community and has touched lives beyond the group itself by bringing hope and enriching lives through art. The most impactful part of PTG has been the kindness, compassion, dedication and understanding that Ms. McCormack brings into the group and prison week after week. Ms. McCormack is a representation of deep empathy and the belief that all people, no matter who you are, or what you have done, deserve a measure of dignity. Ms. McCormack is a true humanitarian going to those living in the shadows, which have no voice, and are outcasts in our society, bringing hope for a better future to those who have little.

What I would like my audience to know about me is that I came into prison as a boy, but I am leaving as a man who knows the meaning of empathy, compassion, and hope. I have made the choices to better my life and have worked hard towards that. I would want you to know that people can change and that people should not be defined by their worst day for the rest of their lives.

Jon Killoran

I enjoy writing as a means of communication, creativity and self-expression. My thanks to Michele and my fellow writers for allowing me the opportunity to partake in the project, as well as for the continued encouragement to improve my craft.

Phillip

I thank Michele for allowing me into her creative writing class Penned Thoughts. This has been a good experience for me. My classmates are very talented, and I admire them and have a lot of respect for them. Every class I learn something about my teacher, my classmates, and myself.

kosal so

"Kosal" means fortunate in Khmer. Born during the reign of Pol Pot, my family became refugees. Before we were able to escape to Thailand, five of my older siblings died. My grandparents were executed and my relatives vanished, never to be heard from again.

My mother took me, the sole survivor, the fortunate one, to a foreign land in hopes of safety and survival. I grew up in Long Beach, California. Before I got a grasp of the English language, I understood what struggle was. That safety and survival are not guaranteed things.

Before I joined a gang, I got jumped a lot. After I joined, the numerous paths ahead of me converged into just two: one headed to the cemetery, one to prison.

Here I sit inside this prison cell, fortunate to be alive. Many years have gone by spent in reflection and reformation. I've discovered that life can be more than about struggle. It can be so beautiful.

I write poetry and make art. Each time I express myself thus, I put a piece of my soul in it, to be liberated. Not just from confinement, but all of life's trappings.

SP

Words help to convey one's true self
Words help to elevate and eviscerate
Words act as a cohesive, solidifying relationship
They're rhythmic, eliciting response from the most dormant of feelings
They're a protector, triggered to defend, at times without a viable threat
They're abundant and dynamic
They are the most powerful tool possessed by this Portland Native
To navigate the ever-changing constructs that confine
Freedumb
Is why I write

HJ Walker

Writing is a gift that all of humanity shares. Through this venue more lives have been liberated than with all the gunpowder in the world. My opinion anyway! Writing started with me in the simple verses of rhythmic poetry. An opportunity where my voice creates a space to express remorse, offer prayers of repentance, shared regrets that we all suffer in life, along with finding hope and dreams for the future. Writing is a safe place where I've appreciated that I am not the sum of my actions.

I grew up with a worldview that life is either black or white thinking. The Penned Thoughts writers' group has given me the courage to break out of those generational cycles of antiquated thought processes, and discover my own self-identity. I have become a unique individual in a world of likes. Without having this space to discover, I would be lost in a sea of humanity. Yes, writing is that powerful for me.

It is important that I be my own man. Not just accepting the existing status quo because that's how things have always been. Writing lets me challenge what I think by the information I possess. Forming my own beliefs about life's tough questions of why I am here and what is my purpose. After all in the end I have to be satisfied with me. In my little insights that I gain, I pray they will encourage others to find their own voice in this avenue of writing.

CPSIA information can be obtained
at www.ICGtesting.com
Printed in the USA
FFOW03n2007150518
46679618-48770FF